# CLASSIC
# HOCKEY
# TRIVIA

## DON WEEKES & KERRY BANKS

D1316624

GREYSTONE BOOKS

DOUGLAS & McINTYRE
VANCOUVER/TORONTO

*For John and Molly Lees. And Mary, Kathy and Jonathan.*—Don Weekes

*For Brian, who faced all those shots in the cellar.*—Kerry Banks

Copyright © 1997 by Don Weekes

98 99 00 01  5 4

All rights reserved. No part of this book may be reproduced, stored in a retrieval system or transmitted in any form or by any means, without the prior permission of the publisher or, in the case of photocopying or other reprographic copying, a licence from CANCOPY (Canadian Reprography Collective), Toronto, Ontario.

Greystone Books
A division of Douglas & McIntyre
1615 Venables Street
Vancouver, British Columbia    V5L 2H1

**Canadian Cataloguing in Publication Data**
Weekes, Don.
    Classic hockey trivia
    ISBN 1-55054-561-2
    1. National Hockey League—Miscellanea. 2. Hockey—Miscellanea. I. Banks, Kerry, 1952- II. Title
GV847.W389 1997    796.962'64    C97-910382-7

Editing by Anne Rose and Kerry Banks
Design by Peter Cocking
Typesetting by Brenda and Neil West, BN Typographics West
Cover photo by Brian Winkler/Bruce Bennett Studios
Printed and bound in Canada by Best Book Manufacturers
Printed on acid-free paper ∞

The publisher gratefully acknowledges the assistance of the Canada Council for the Arts and of the British Columbia Ministry of Tourism, Small Business and Culture.

*Don Weekes is a television producer and writer with CFCF 12 in Montreal. This is his ninth hockey trivia quiz book.*

*Kerry Banks is an award-winning magazine features writer, a sports columnist and TV sports commentator, and the author of baseball and hockey trivia books. He lives in Vancouver.*

# CONTENTS

# PREFACE

There were many big hockey stories in 1996-97, but none bigger than the retirement of Mario Lemieux. He kept us guessing about his intentions, almost until the 1997 playoffs, as if he wasn't sure if this was the right time to leave the game. Lemieux was only 31, and though he didn't add another Stanley Cup to go with his two previous championships in his last season, he went out on top as a player, winning his sixth NHL scoring title and notching his 600th career goal.

The chronic back pain, the various injuries and the bout with cancer that sidelined Lemieux for lengthy stretches throughout his career may have diminished his scoring stats, but they only added to his legend as he rebounded from adversity stronger each time. After missing 24 games while undergoing radiation treatment for Hodgkin's disease in 1992-93, Lemieux came back to score an astounding 160 points in just 60 games, capturing the Hart Trophy as the NHL's top scorer and the Hart Trophy as MVP.

Lemieux retired for his own reasons, and the ending was in true Lemieux fashion, memorable. It was especially dramatic in Montreal, his hometown, and in Pittsburgh, the home of the Penguins (the only pro team he had ever played for). At his final appearance in Montreal's Molson Centre, Lemieux recorded five points, including two third-period goals. After the last one, the crowd awarded him with a long and thunderous ovation. He said later it was the greatest thanks he could have received. In his final shift at Pittsburgh's Civic Arena in the first round of the playoffs, he scored on a breakaway against Flyers goalie Garth Snow with 1:04 left in the third period. When he was named the game's first star, Lemieux came out and circled the ice one last time, waving and blowing kisses to the cheering throng. He wept in the dressing room after the game.

Hockey has been blessed by another magnificent talent. Adieu, Mario.

DON WEEKES, KERRY BANKS
July 1997

# 1

# THE FIRST SHIFT

Gordie Howe scored in his first game in 1946; Wayne Gretzky recorded the first of thousands of points in his first NHL contest. But how many players have scored on their first shift? Among 5,500 NHLers, only a handful can lay claim to that feat, including Danny Gare, Alexander Mogilny and Mario Lemieux (Lemieux scored his first goal on his first shot of his first shift of his first game). Consider this chapter on general trivia your first shift in the big leagues. Sure, you may not have all the answers, but the trick is to pick the multiple-choice option that fits best.

*(Answers are on page 6)*

**1.1** **In 1996-97, Mario Lemieux reached the 600-goal milestone faster than any player in NHL annals except Wayne Gretzky. How many more games than Gretzky did it take Lemieux to reach number 600?**
A. One game
B. Six games
C. 66 games
D. 99 games

**1.2** **Which NHL sniper has Japanese ancestry?**
A. Joe Juneau
B. Alexei Yashin
C. Paul Kariya
D. Mike Modano

**1.3** **Canadian astronaut Robert Thirsk took whose hockey sweater and Stanley Cup ring into orbit on a 1996 shuttle mission?**
A. Joe Sakic's
B. Wayne Gretzky's
C. Bobby Orr's
D. Patrick Roy's

**1.4** Which defenseman reached 1,000 career points in the fewest games?
A. Denis Potvin
B. Paul Coffey
C. Ray Bourque
D. Bobby Orr

**1.5** In December 1996, *The Hockey News* had a panel of pro scouts evaluate NHL players in five categories: size, skill, skating, spirit and hockey sense. Who received the highest cumulative score?
A. Eric Lindros
B. Jaromir Jagr
C. Peter Forsberg
D. Patrick Roy

**1.6** In 1996, the Supreme Court of Canada ruled that more than 1,300 NHLers would receive lump-sum payments for misappropriated pension money collected by the league between 1947 and 1982. Gordie Howe, who played for 26 years, received the largest award: $205,005. How much money did Neal Broten get for his 76 games from 1980 to 1982?
A. $55.15
B. $555.15
C. $5,555.15
D. $55,555.15

**1.7** Who was the first hockey player to have his image appear on a Campbell's soup can?
A. Jean Béliveau
B. Gordie Howe
C. Wayne Gretzky
D. Darryl Sittler

**1.8** Which NHL player made a miraculous return to action in 1996-97, only eight months after undergoing brain surgery?
A. Donald Audette
B. Kris Draper
C. Mike Ridley
D. Tony Granato

**1.9** According to recent surveys, how many NHL players wear helmets that fail to meet the safety guidelines set by the Canadian Standards Association?
A. 10 per cent
B. 20 per cent
C. 30 per cent
D. 40 per cent

**1.10** As of 1996-97, which two NHL teams had recorded the most 100-point seasons?
A. Boston and Montreal
B. Montreal and Philadelphia
C. Philadelphia and Boston
D. Edmonton and Montreal

**1.11** In 1996, which NHL club became the first professional hockey team to be traded on the stock exchange?
A. The Boston Bruins
B. The Florida Panthers
C. The Dallas Stars
D. The Colorado Avalanche

**1.12** Which NHL team's scoreboard crashed to the ice prior to a game in 1996-97?
A. The San Jose Sharks'
B. The Buffalo Sabres'
C. The Calgary Flames'
D. The Washington Capitals'

**1.13** Tampa Bay's Alexander Selivanov blamed his slow start in 1996-97 on his club's new arena. What did Selivanov say was wrong with the Ice Palace?
A. The ice was bad
B. The lights were too bright
C. The music was distracting
D. The arena was haunted

**1.14** What was the name of the fictional minor-league hockey team that the Hanson brothers played for in the 1977 film *Slap Shot*?

A. The Dayton Daggers
B. The Wheeling Wildcats
C. The Charleston Chiefs
D. The Nashville Knights

**1.15** In which NHL arena will you never see a Zamboni?

A. Pittsburgh's Civic Arena
B. Montreal's Molson Centre
C. Vancouver's General Motors Place
D. Detroit's Joe Louis Arena

**1.16** Who is John Paris, Jr.?

A. Eric Lindros's bodyguard
B. The inventor of the FoxTrax puck
C. The first black pro hockey coach
D. The NHL's official statistician

**1.17** Pavel Bure revived an old family business in Russia in 1996. What was the business?

A. Vodka distilling
B. Watchmaking
C. Hockey-stick manufacturing
D. Sable farming

**1.18** Who were the first brothers voted to the NHL's First All-Star Team in the same year?

A. Maurice and Henri Richard
B. Phil and Tony Esposito
C. Doug and Max Bentley
D. Charlie and Lionel Conacher

1.19 Which sportswear manufacturer produced television commercials with fictional down-on-their-luck goalies in 1997?
A. Easton
B. Nike
C. Starter
D. CCM

1.20 A vocal cord injury prevents which NHL defenseman from hollering to his teammates on the ice?
A. Chris Pronger
B. Mark Tinordi
C. Dave Manson
D. Robert Svehla

1.21 In 1996-97, who was the highest-paid NHL coach?
A. Detroit's Scotty Bowman
B. Colorado's Marc Crawford
C. Los Angeles' Larry Robinson
D. New Jersey's Jacques Lemaire

1.22 Which rock star was the inspiration for the naming of the Jacksonville Lizard Kings of the East Coast Hockey League?
A. Gene Simmons
B. Ozzy Osbourne
C. Jim Morrison
D. Alice Cooper

1.23 In 1996-97, Bobby Carpenter became the fifth American-born player to play 1,000 games in the NHL. Who was the first American to reach the 1,000-game milestone?
A. Gordie Roberts
B. Neal Broten
C. Joe Mullen
D. Mike Ramsey

**1.24** All NHL teams now play on regulation-size (200-by-85-foot) rinks. Which was the last undersize rink in the NHL?
A. Chicago Stadium
B. Boston Garden
C. The Detroit Olympia
D. Buffalo's War Memorial Auditorium

**1.25** Who wrote the theme for the CBC's *Hockey Night in Canada*?
A. Canadian singer/songwriter Paul Anka
B. Jingle composer Dolores Claman
C. Canadian country singer Stompin' Tom Connors
D. Amateur songwriter Billy Cochrane, who won a write-in contest

# THE FIRST SHIFT
## *Answers*

**1.1 A. One game**

Lemieux needed only one more game than Gretzky to notch his 600th career goal. Gretzky scored number 600 in his 718th regular-season game. Lemieux's milestone marker, an empty-netter, came in his 719th game—a 6-4 Penguins home-ice win against the Vancouver Canucks, February 5, 1997. When Lemieux slid the puck into the net, the Civic Arena's packed crowd of 17,355 erupted with cheers and littered the ice with hats. Lemieux said he was honoured to be part of the 600 club. "It's a pretty special list. You look at the names: Esposito, Dionne, Gretzky, guys like that. To be included on the list is something I'll be able to cherish the rest of my life."

**1.2 C. Paul Kariya**

Kariya's grandparents on his father's side are Japanese. During World War II, they suffered the fate of many of North America's Japanese immigrants: they were stripped of their belongings and sent to internment camps, because they were considered a potential threat to the government. Isamu and Fumiko Kariya spent more than five years in custody in Greenwood, British Columbia,

Canada. It was here that Paul's father, Tetsuhiko, was born. Kariya's Japanese ancestry is bound to make him a major story when the Canadian Olympic hockey team competes at the 1998 Winter Olympics in Nagano, Japan.

### 1.3   C. Bobby Orr's

A blood-spattered Boston Bruins jersey of Orr's and one of the hockey legend's **Stanley Cup** rings were among the mementoes that blasted off with Canadian astronaut Robert Thirsk on the space shuttle *Columbia* in June 1996. Although the two men had never met, Thirsk admitted that Orr was always his hero. Shortly before embarking on his space adventure, "I finally got the nerve to call him up and ask him, out of respect, if I could fly something for him," said Thirsk. The astronaut, who assumed Orr's choice would be something of little value, was amazed when a package arrived containing Orr's diamond-studded 1970 Stanley Cup ring with the famous "No. 4" engraved on it. More surprising, it came via regular mail. A few days later, Thirsk received another parcel from Orr containing one of his game-worn jerseys.

### 1.4   B. Paul Coffey

Coffey notched his 1,000th NHL point in his 770th regular-season game, reaching the milestone in 163 games less than his closest pursuer, Ray Bourque. Bobby Orr likely would have been the fastest D-man to reach the millennium mark if he had stayed healthy for another season. Orr retired in 1978-79, after scoring 915 points in only 657 games. Phil Housley and Al MacInnis will both crack the 1,000-point barrier, but neither one is anywhere close to doing it as quickly as Coffey.

| The NHL's 1,000-Point Defensemen* | | | |
|---|---|---|---|
| **Player** | **Team** | **Date** | **Game No.** |
| Paul Coffey | Pittsburgh | 12/22/90 | 770 |
| Ray Bourque | Boston | 02/29/92 | 933 |
| Denis Potvin | NYI | 04/04/87 | 987 |
| Larry Murphy | Toronto | 03/27/96 | 1,228 |
| *Current to 1997 | | | |

**1.5   D.   Patrick Roy**

The Colorado Avalanche netminder scored 24 out of a possible 25 points in *The Hockey News* survey, the highest score of the 607 players evaluated. Jaromir Jagr, Peter Forsberg and Chris Chelios finished in a three-way tie for second with a score of 23.5.

**1.6   A.   $55.15**

The pension payouts to 1,343 players were calculated on years of service, pension contributions and age. A total of 56 retired players received more than $100,000. Others, including Mike Gartner and Dave Semenko, got less than $10,000. Broten, who entered the league full-time during the last year of eligibility (1981-82), collected just $55.15.

**1.7   C.   Wayne Gretzky**

The term superstar took on a new meaning for Wayne Gretzky in 1996-97, when he became the first person to appear on a Campbell's soup label. The image of Gretzky—clad in a generic hockey uniform—along with his signature, appeared on 50 million labels of 20 different varieties of Campbell's Chunky soup.

**1.8   D.   Tony Granato**

After sliding headfirst into the boards during a game against the Hartford Whalers on January 25, 1995, the Los Angeles Kings winger began experiencing severe headaches and loss of memory. Medical tests revealed that Granato needed brain surgery. On February 14, 1995, he underwent a four-hour operation to remove an abnormal swelling on the left side of his brain. The surgery was successful. A few months later, Granato's doctors told him he could resume his career. He signed as a free agent with the San Jose Sharks in August and returned to action at the start of the 1996-97 season. In his second game, Granato scored a hat trick against his former team, the Kings.

**1.9   C.   30 per cent**

Three out of 10 NHL skaters on every shift wear helmets that don't meet the impact standards set by the Canadian Standards

Association, a nonprofit organization that evaluates product safety. According to the CSA, helmets should have five-eighths of an inch of padding to give adequate protection. Unfortunately, many players wear helmets with far less padding, including Wayne Gretzky, Igor Larionov and Esa Tikkanen. As Islanders team doctor Elliot Pellman told *Sports Illustrated* in 1996, "Some guys are wearing helmets that are so poor you might as well put a baggie over their heads." This reluctance to don proper headgear is a factor in the alarming number of head injuries suffered by NHLers. In 1995-96 alone, 70 players received concussions.

### 1.10  A.  Boston and Montreal

As of 1997, the Bruins and Canadiens were deadlocked for most 100-point seasons. Both clubs had reached the century mark 15 times. The next best teams were Philadelphia (12), the Islanders (7), Buffalo, Chicago, Edmonton (6) and the Rangers (5). Which year produced the most 100-point clubs? A record seven teams hit the mark in 1992-93.

### 1.11  B.  The Florida Panthers

Panthers owner Wayne Huizenga claimed to have lost $25 million on his hockey club in 1995, but he turned a losing venture into a profitable one in a single day. In November 1996, Huizenga sold nearly six million shares in the Panthers, (49 per cent of the team), at prices that fluctuated between U.S.$12 and U.S.$14 a share. In total, he reaped U.S.$67.3 million for the team, which had been valued at U.S.$45 million by *Financial World* magazine. The Boston Celtics, the other major-league team whose shares are publicly traded, is valued at U.S.$125 million on the stock market.

### 1.12  B.  The Buffalo Sabres'

On November 16, 1996, a cable snapped as the $4.5-million, eight-sided scoreboard at Buffalo's new Marine Midland Arena was being lowered during a routine afternoon maintenance check, sending the four-ton structure crashing to the ice. Luckily, no one was on the rink at the time. The ice was not damaged, but the state-of-the-art scoreboard shattered on impact. The mishap forced the cancellation of that night's game, between the Sabres and the Boston Bruins.

### 1.13 D. The arena was haunted

After Selivanov scored 31 goals to lead the Lightning in 1995-96, Tampa Bay expected big things from him in 1996-97. When the Russian winger scored only once in the team's first nine home games, reporters asked him what the problem was. The superstitious Selivanov had a novel excuse. He claimed Tampa Bay's new arena was haunted, based on the fact that the Ice Palace was built atop the graves of pre-Civil War soldiers. "They find bones here," said Selivanov in broken English. "Who knows, Ice Palace cursed maybe. Something wrong. I don't understand it."

### 1.14 C. The Charleston Chiefs

The 1977 comedy *Slap Shot* starred Paul Newman as the playing coach of the Charlestown Chiefs, a hapless minor-league hockey team that achieves success thanks to the violent antics of a trio of bespectacled goons known as the Hanson brothers. Not only were the actors who portrayed the Hansons real hockey players, Newman's character, Reg Dunlop, was modelled on John Brophy, a playing coach with the Johnstown Jets of the old Eastern Hockey League. The silver-haired Brophy later coached the Toronto Maple Leafs in the 1980s. Some may be surprised to learn that *Slap Shot*'s raunchy script was penned by a woman, Nancy Dowd. She was aided in her realistic grasp of jock banter by her brother, Ned, a player with the Johnstown Jets, who sneaked a tape recorder on the team bus.

### 1.15 C. Vancouver's General Motors Place

Orca Bay, the company that owns the Vancouver arena and the Canucks, is not allowed to use a Zamboni under the terms of its sponsorship contract with General Motors. Instead, a GM machine called an Olympia performs the ice-cleaning duties.

## 1.16  C.  The first black pro hockey coach

Although far from a household name, John Paris, Jr. has impressive credentials to go with the distinction of being the first black coach in pro hockey. In his 24 years behind the bench, Paris has been named top coach in five different hockey leagues. After transforming the Atlanta Knights of the International Hockey League into a contender, Paris assumed the coaching reins of the expansion Macon Whoopee of the Central League in 1996-97. Although the Whoopee roster had 12 first-year players, Paris guided them to a second-place finish in the CHL's Eastern Division. The Whoopee were defeated in the first round of the CHL playoffs by Memphis.

## 1.17  B.  Watchmaking

In 1996, Pavel Bure decided to revive the family watchmaking business founded by his great, great, great grandfather in Czarist Russia. The business venture made headlines, but for all the wrong reasons. ESPNEWS reported that Bure's business partner, Anzor Kikalichvili, was a member of the Russian mafia, involved with money laundering, extortion and drug dealing. Bure denied the report.

## 1.18  D.  Charlie and Lionel Conacher

Only two brother combos have been elected to the NHL's First All-Star Team in the same year. The Conachers were the first to do it. In 1934, Lionel of the Blackhawks earned a berth on defense, while Charlie of the Maple Leafs claimed the right-wing spot. Phil and Tony Esposito managed the feat twice, in 1970 and 1972. Maurice and Henri Richard and Doug and Max Bentley were voted to the first All-Star team during their careers, but never in the same year.

## 1.19  B.  Nike

The four hockey ads with fictitious down-and-out goalies were created by Nike, the planet's largest athletic apparel retailer. Nike got into hockey in 1994 by buying Canadian-owned Canstar, the makers of Bauer skates and Cooper pads. Ever since, the Nike ad men have pitched their hockey products just like their court gear: hype a superstar in artful over-the-top campaigns that sell "cool" and redefine "attitude" for every kid watching. Nike's hockey ads focus on four former NHL goalies (in full gear) whose careers were ruined after their "weak glove hand" or "weak stick hand" was exposed by the likes of Mats Sundin, Sergei Fedorov or Jeremy Roenick, and "the effortless way he skates the puck through traffic . . . in his shiny Nike skates." Each unemployed goalie now works either as a janitor, a panhandler, a burger flipper or, in the most hilarious scenario, a French-Canadian cabbie who drives even more badly than he tends goal.

## 1.20 C. Dave Manson

The saying "Speak softly and carry a big stick" accurately describes Dave Manson. The rugged Habs rearguard is one of the NHL's more intimidating players, but to hear Manson speak you have to stand close to him. Manson's voice was damaged after he was punched in the throat by Sergio Momesso during a 1991 fight. The blow crushed Manson's vocal cords, leaving him with a gravelly rasp. A 1994 operation failed to correct the problem, and Manson continues to play without being able to verbally communicate with his teammates on the ice.

## 1.21 D. New Jersey's Jacques Lemaire

While players have long reaped the benefits of salary disclosure, it wasn't until the 1996 NHL Entry Draft that coaches gathered for the first time and revealed how much or (sometimes) how little they make. Although wary of such a public forum, each coach stood and announced his salary and bonuses to the others. The meeting revealed "inconsistencies in the way coaches are treated in our business," said Scotty Bowman. So what's a coach worth? If, as Marc Crawford suggests, "players are 90 per cent responsible for wins and losses . . . and coaching is worth five to 10 per cent," then shouldn't coaching get that proportion of a club's total budget? According to *The Hockey News*, the highest-paid NHL coach in 1996-97 was Jacques Lemaire, who earned $750,000 per year—nowhere near 10 per cent of the Devils' $26.1-million payroll.

## 1997's Top and Bottom Salaries of NHL Coaches

| | Coach | Team | Age | Years | Salary |
|---|---|---|---|---|---|
| 1. | Jacques Lemaire | New Jersey | 51 | 6 | $750,000 |
| 2. | Marc Crawford | Colorado | 35 | 3 | $700,000 |
| 3. | Mike Milbury | NYI | 44 | 4 | $700,000 |
| 4. | Scotty Bowman | Detroit | 63 | 25 | $650,000 |
| 5. | Larry Robinson | Los Angeles | 45 | 2 | $550,000 |
| 22. | Mario Tremblay | Montreal | 40 | 2 | $260,000 |
| 23. | Paul Maurice | Hartford | 30 | 2 | $250,000 |
| 24. | Al Sims | San Jose | 43 | 1 | $250,000 |
| 25. | Jacques Martin | Ottawa | 44 | 4 | $241,000 |
| 26. | Tom Renney | Vancouver | 41 | 1 | $223,000 |

### 1.22  C.  Jim Morrison

As hockey moves deeper into the American sunbelt, all kinds of odd creatures are turning up in team names. At last count, we had the Amarillo Rattlers, New Mexico Scorpions, South Carolina Stingrays, Orlando Solar Bears and Louisville Riverfrogs. Larry Lane, owner of Jacksonville's 1996-97 entry in the ECHL, called his team the Lizard Kings as a tribute to his favourite rock star. Jim Morrison, charismatic singer/poet of The Doors, had a fascination with dreams, death and insanity and often used these themes in his lyrics, especially in his poem "Celebration of the Lizard" ("I am the Lizard King, I can do anything"). Clad in black leather and slithering on stage, Morrison became the Lizard King for a generation of music fans.

### 1.23  A.  Gordie Roberts

Detroit-born Roberts reached the 1,000-game milestone in 1992-93. He played 1,097 games during his 16-year career, which included stints in Hartford, Minnesota, Philadelphia, St. Louis, Pittsburgh and Boston. Mike Ramsey and Neal Broten reached the mark in 1994-95; Joe Mullen in 1995-96.

## 1.24 D. Buffalo's War Memorial Auditorium

The opening of Buffalo's new Marine Midland Center in 1996-97 spelled the end for the last of the NHL's undersize rinks. War Memorial Auditorium measured 84 by 193 feet. Other small rinks that were recently phased out include Boston Garden (83 by 191 feet) and the Chicago Stadium (85 by 185 feet). Those two rinks were smaller than regulation size because they were built before the NHL passed legislation in 1929-30, requiring all rinks to have ice surfaces measuring 200 by 85 feet. When the Sabres joined the NHL in 1970, they moved into War Memorial Auditorium, which was built in 1940. The club received special permission to play on a smaller ice surface, provided it increased the arena's seating capacity from 10,000 to 15,000.

## 1.25 B. Jingle composer Dolores Claman

Da En Da En Da Da Naaa. So familiar is Claman's opening to *Hockey Night in Canada* that it has been called Canada's unofficial national anthem. Playing each Saturday night in hockey season since 1967, the theme has been indelibly etched into the Canadian consciousness. The producers of HNIC asked Claman to write a big, brassy opener like the popular themes from American action TV shows of the 1960s (e.g., *Mission Impossible*). Claman submitted two potential musical lead-ins. The CBC's pick has been HNIC's signature tune ever since.

# GAME 1
# JUSTICE FOR ALL

In April 1991, seven retired NHLers filed a $40-million lawsuit against the league for misappropriation of pension monies (and interest) collected by the league between 1947 and 1982. After a five-year court battle, 1,343 players, including Gordie Howe, Bobby Hull and Billy Harris (three of the orginal seven complainants), received lump-sum payments based on years of service, pension contributions and age. Considering Howe's longevity, the Detroit superstar was entitled to the largest sum, more than $200,000. Factoring in years of service and salary scales between 1947 and 1982, guess how much money the players below recovered due to the 1996 Supreme Court of Canada ruling.

*(Solutions are on page 111)*

| $6,917 | $7,083 | $14,835 | $21,612 | $36,376 |
|---|---|---|---|---|
| $59,043 | $69,311 | $77,465 | $91,072 | $106,411 |
| $128,002 | $148,756 | $164,837 | $184,901 | |

| If ... | got ... | then ... | got ... |
|---|---|---|---|
| Gordie Howe | $205,005, | Gump Worsley | $_____ |
| Tony Esposito | $94,494, | Phil Esposito | $_____ |
| Larry Robinson | $26,841, | Ray Bourque | $_____ |
| Eddie Shack | $125,955, | John Ferguson | $_____ |
| Joel Quenneville | $9,961, | Jacques Lemaire | $_____ |
| Serge Savard | $90,485, | Denis Potvin | $_____ |
| Gerry Cheevers | $86,814, | Eddie Johnston | $_____ |
| Bryan Trottier | $23,544, | Mike Bossy | $_____ |
| Ken Dryden | $43,432, | Bobby Orr | $_____ |
| Brian Propp | $7,701, | Charlie Simmer | $_____ |
| Jean Béliveau | $132,161, | Bobby Hull | $_____ |
| Alex Delvecchio | $154,760, | Ron Ellis | $_____ |
| Frank Mahovlich | $121,316, | Stan Mikita | $_____ |
| Wayne Gretzky | $6,917, | Mark Messier | $_____ |

# 2

# TRIGGERMEN

It's often said that the one hockey skill that can't be taught is goal scoring. Though players can improve the speed and accuracy of their shots with practise, the intangibles that set the elite scorers apart—soft hands, poise and a sixth sense of anticipation—are natural gifts. When these snipers get an opportunity they usually bury the puck. In this chapter, we go one-on-one with some of hockey's deadliest triggermen.

*(Answers are on page 19)*

2.1 **Who was the first American-born player to lead the NHL in goal scoring?**
A. Pat LaFontaine
B. Keith Tkachuk
C. Mike Modano
D. John LeClair

2.2 **Who entered the record books in 1996-97 by becoming the first NHLer to score all five of his team's goals in a regular-season game?**
A. Paul Kariya
B. Peter Bondra
C. Zigmund Palffy
D. Sergei Fedorov

2.3 **In NHL history, there have only been about 60 games where one player has scored five or more goals. What is the most times an NHLer has managed a five-or-more-goal game?**
A. Two times
B. Three times
C. Four times
D. Five times

**2.4** During 1996-97, Wayne Gretzky experienced the longest goal drought of his career. How many straight games did Gretzky go without scoring a goal?
A. 11
B. 16
C. 21
D. 26

**2.5** In what league did Wayne Gretzky produce the greatest margin of points between himself and the next best player?
A. In minor hockey
B. In junior hockey
C. In the WHA
D. In the NHL

**2.6** Which NHL gunner scored his 50th goal of the season on his birthday?
A. Mike Bossy
B. Guy Lafleur
C. Phil Esposito
D. Wayne Gretzky

**2.7** Which high-scoring forward is nicknamed "Killer"?
A. Mike Modano
B. Doug Gilmour
C. Daniel Alfredsson
D. Keith Tkachuk

**2.8** Whose NHL rookie scoring record did Gilbert Perreault break when he tallied 72 points for the Buffalo Sabres in 1970-71?
A. Toronto's Howie Meeker
B. Montreal's Bernie Geoffrion
C. Chicago's Bill Mosienko
D. Toronto's Frank Mahovlich

**2.9** Besides Bobby Orr and Paul Coffey, how many other NHL defensemen have recorded 100-point seasons?
A. None
B. One
C. Two
D. Three

**2.10** Who holds the NHL mark for most power-play goals in a season?
A. Tim Kerr
B. Brett Hull
C. Mario Lemieux
D. Dave Andreychuk

**2.11** Which NHL sniper was "kidnapped" by his pals and taken on a wild, two-day bachelor party just before his marriage in 1996?
A. Tony Amonte
B. Keith Tkachuk
C. Geoff Sanderson
D. Teemu Selanne

**2.12** No pair of teammates has ever dominated the NHL scoring chart like Phil Esposito and Bobby Orr of the Boston Bruins. How many seasons did they rank one-two in the points parade?
A. Four
B. Five
C. Six
D. Seven

**2.13** Who holds the modern-era NHL mark for scoring the highest percentage of his team's goals in a season?
A. Toronto's Frank Mahovlich
B. Montreal's Maurice Richard
C. St. Louis' Brett Hull
D. Pittsburgh's Mario Lemieux

2.14 The first NHL sharpshooter to notch 70 goals in a season was Phil Esposito; the second was Wayne Gretzky. Who was the third player to reach the 70-goal plateau?
A. Edmonton's Jari Kurri
B. The Islanders' Mike Bossy
C. Pittsburgh's Mario Lemieux
D. Los Angeles' Bernie Nicholls

2.15 Who is the only player to count five points in his first NHL game?
A. New York's Don Murdoch
B. Philadelphia's Al Hill
C. Pittsburgh's Mike Bullard
D. St. Louis' Bernie Federko

2.16 Who is the oldest NHLer to score 50 goals in a season?
A. Johnny Bucyk
B. Joe Mullen
C. Phil Esposito
D. Marcel Dionne

# TRIGGERMEN
## *Answers*

2.1 **B. Keith Tkachuk**
The NHL goal-scoring race has been won by Finns, Czechs, Russians and, of course, Canadians. Yet, not until 1996-97, when Melrose, Massachusetts, native Keith Tkachuk netted 52 goals, did a U.S.-born player top all NHL goal scorers. Right behind Tkachuk were Finn Teemu Selanne (51), Canadian Mario Lemieux (50) and fellow American John LeClair (50). (Brett Hull, who won three goal-scoring titles in the early 1990s, is Canadian born.)

2.2 **D. Sergei Fedorov**
The Russian Red Wing had a subpar season in 1996-97, but on December 26, against Washington, Fedorov showed a blinding flash of brilliance. He scored five goals, including one in

overtime, to carry Detroit to a 5-4 victory. "My arms were almost numb on the third and fourth goals," said Fedorov after the game. "I just made sure I wasn't shaking and hit the puck hard (on the fifth goal) like a golf swing." It marked the first time in NHL annals that a player had scored all five of his team's goals in a regular-season game.

## 2.3 D. Five times

"Phantom" Joe Malone kicked off his NHL career in 1917-18 with a bang, netting five goals in his first game with the Montreal Canadiens. The goal explosion was a sign of things to come. Although he only played 125 NHL regular-season games, the stylish forward potted 146 goals. Multigoal games were Malone's specialty. He scored three goals or more 47 times in his 16-year pro career. His NHL tally included three five-goal games, one six-goal game and one seven-goal game. Malone's seven-goal explosion against the Toronto St. Pats on January 31, 1920, remains an NHL record. Wayne Gretzky, the only player to come close to Malone's mark, has scored five goals in a game on four occasions.

## 2.4 C. 21

There was nothing wrong with Wayne Gretzky's assist production with the New York Rangers in 1996-97 (72 assists), but during a 21-game span in midseason the NHL's greatest goal scorer could not *buy* a goal. The longest drought of Gretzky's career finally ended on February 21, against Hartford, when he drifted a long, harmless-looking shot at the net that eluded goalie Sean Burke. Although the goal lifted a weight off Gretzky's shoulders, it didn't help the Rangers, who lost 7-2.

## 2.5 A. In minor hockey

As a nine-year-old in 1970-71 with the Brantford Nadrofsky Steelers of the Ontario Minor Hockey Association, Gretzky scored 196 goals and 120 assists in 76 games. "He'll never do that again," people said. They were right. The next season the wonderboy racked up an astounding 378 goals and 139 assists for 517 points in 69 games. That season Gretzky won the scoring race by 238 goals.

### 2.6  C. Phil Esposito

The Boston sniper hit the 50-goal mark not once, not twice, but three times on his birthday—a truly unusual hat trick! Obviously, Esposito's midwinter birthdate of February 20 is a contributing factor. For example, Guy Lafleur, who was born on September 20, had no chance of duplicating this feat. Even so, the stunt still qualifies as a fascinating oddity. Espo did it in 1971, 1972 and 1974.

### 2.7  B. Doug Gilmour

Gilmour was given the nickname early in his career by his former Blues teammate Brian Sutter. Sutter began calling Gilmour "Killer" because of the fierce look in Gilmour's eyes. Few NHLers play with more desire or intensity than Gilmour, who is listed at 185 pounds but plays at about 165, soaking wet.

### 2.8  C. Chicago's Bill Mosienko

Mosienko, who is best known for the fastest hat trick in NHL history (three goals in 21 seconds), established a new NHL record for points by a rookie when he collected 70 points with the Chicago Blackhawks in 1943-44. Mosienko's mark would stand for 27 years until Gilbert Perreault broke it in 1970-71. However, Perreault played 78 games that season, while Mosienko set his standard in a 50-game schedule.

### 2.9  D. Three

Bobby Orr recorded an amazing six 100-point seasons while Paul Coffey did it five times, which puts them in a category above even today's most offensive D-men. For most NHL rearguards, 100 points remains an almost unattainable goal. As of 1996-97, only three other defensemen had topped the plateau and all three barely made it. Denis Potvin netted 101 points in 1978-79; Al MacInnis notched 103 points in 1990-91; and Brian Leetch tallied 102 points in 1991-92.

### 2.10  A. Tim Kerr

During the 1980s, Kerr was dubbed "the human slot machine" for his uncanny knack of scoring from the slot in front of the net. At six foot three and 230 pounds, he was almost impossible to move once he had planted himself at his customary post. The big centre topped the 50-goal mark four straight seasons in the 1980s with the Philadelphia Flyers. Kerr was especially deadly on the power play. His 34 power-play goals in 1985-86 remains an NHL record.

**Most Power-Play Goals in a Season***

| Player | Year | Team | Goals |
|--------|------|------|-------|
| Tim Kerr | 1985-86 | Phi | 34 |
| Dave Andreychuk | 1992-93 | Tor | 32 |
| Mario Lemieux | 1995-96 | Pit | 31 |
| Mario Lemieux | 1988-89 | Pit | 31 |
| Joe Nieuwendyk | 1987-88 | Cal | 31 |

*Current to 1997*

## 2.11 D. Teemu Selanne

A couple of days before the fun-loving Finn and his wife were married in Helsinki, on July 19, 1996, more than 20 of Selanne's pals slapped him into a pair of handcuffs, blindfolded him and took him on a rollicking, two-day bachelor party. Before the romp was over, Selanne had been paraded about town dressed like Elvis and had had one of his legs tattooed with a yellow lightning bolt, superimposed over a Finnish flag. Later, he was blindfolded again, given a change of clothes and ear plugs and driven around for an hour with the car stereo blaring at full volume. When the car was finally stopped and Selanne's blindfold removed, he found himself standing in a soccer stadium in front of 10,000 screaming fans. He was wearing the home uniform of Helsinki Finnpa, a team in Finland's elite soccer league. Selanne, who played in the game and almost scored a goal, described the entire experience as "great."

## 2.12 B. Five

Esposito and Orr finished one-two in the NHL scoring race five times in six seasons (1969-70 to 1974-75). During that span,

Esposito topped the chart four times and Orr twice. Boston's dynamic duo would have been six for six if not for the Flyers' Bobby Clarke, who edged Orr for second place in 1972-73 by three points, 104 to 101. Orr would have undoubtedly finished ahead of Clarke had he not missed 15 games with injuries. In fact, Orr would have given Espo a run for first.

## 2.13 C. St. Louis' Brett Hull

No modern-day NHLer has contributed as much firepower to his team's offense as Hull did with St. Louis in 1990-91 and 1991-92. His 86-goal barrage in 1990-91 was more than 27 per cent of the Blues' total output. It was also 35 goals more than any other NHLer scored that year, another league record. Though Hull only popped 70 the next year, it still amounted to 25 per cent of St. Louis' offense. Those two seasons rank one-two for highest percentage of a team's goals in a season.

### Highest Percentage of Team Goals in a Season*

| Player | Year | Team | Goals | Team Goals | PCT |
|---|---|---|---|---|---|
| Brett Hull | 1990-91 | StL | 86 | 310 | 27.7 |
| Brett Hull | 1991-92 | StL | 70 | 279 | 25.1 |
| Maurice Richard | 1949-50 | Mtl | 43 | 172 | 25.0 |
| Peter Bondra | 1994-95 | Was | 34 | 136 | 25.0 |
| Mario Lemieux | 1988-89 | Pit | 85 | 347 | 24.5 |
| Brett Hull | 1989-90 | StL | 72 | 295 | 24.4 |
| Maurice Richard | 1950-51 | Mtl | 42 | 173 | 24.3 |

*Since 1942

## 2.14 A. Edmonton's Jari Kurri

The Finnish sharpshooter became the NHL's third 70-goal man in 1984-85, when he lit the lamp 71 times with the Oilers. Kurri continued to sizzle in the playoffs, notching a record four hat tricks against Chicago in the semifinals and equalling Reggie Leach's all-time mark of 19 goals in one playoff year.

## 2.15 B. Philadelphia's Al Hill

Al Hill kept mumbling, "I can't believe it. I can't believe it." The rookie's state of disbelief was understandable. Hill had just scored a record five points for the Flyers in his NHL debut on February 14, 1977. Called up earlier that day from the AHL's Springfield Indians, Hill wasted no time getting on the scoreboard, blasting a 45-footer past St. Louis Blues goalie Yves Belanger only 36 seconds into the first period. Hill scored again on his second shot just 11 minutes later, and went on to add three assists in the Flyers' 6-4 win. Oddly, Hill was never able to duplicate his first-game magic. He scored just one point in eight more games that season and was sent back to Springfield. Hill bounced back and forth between the Flyers and the minors for eight seasons, collecting an NHL career total of 95 points.

## 2.16 A. Johnny Bucyk

Like fine wine, Bucyk seemed to improve with age. He enjoyed his best offensive campaign at age 35, in his 16th NHL season, when he compiled 116 points on 51 goals and 65 assists. No other player has reached the 50-goal mark at the "advanced age" of 35. The Boston left-winger continued to fill the net until age 42, when he retired with a career total of 556 goals.

### The NHL's Oldest 50-Goal Scorers*

| Player | Team | Year | Age | Goals |
|---|---|---|---|---|
| Johnny Bucyk | Bos | 70-71 | 35 years/10 months | 51 |
| Phil Esposito | Bos | 74-75 | 33 years/0 months | 61 |
| Joe Mullen | Cal | 88-89 | 32 years/1 month | 51 |
| Marcel Dionne | LA | 82-83 | 31 years/8 months | 56 |
| Vic Hadfield | NYR | 71-72 | 31 years/6 months | 50 |
| Mario Lemieux | Pit | 96-97 | 31 years/6 months | 50 |
| Dave Andreychuk | Tor | 93-94 | 30 years/6 months | 53 |

*Current to 1997

# GAME 2

# THE ORIGINS OF STARS

The most profound change in hockey has been the explosion in the diversity of the birthplaces of players. In 1967, 97 per cent of all NHLers were born in Canada, only 2 per cent were born in the United States and 1 per cent were born outside North America. In 1997, Canadians made up 60 per cent of the league's player population, 20 per cent were American born and 20 per cent were European. Some prospects are signed to teams as free agents, but most NHLers are drafted from Canada's three junior leagues (the OHL, QMJHL and WHL), United States colleges and high schools, European leagues and other North American leagues. In this game, match the NHL stars and their amateur teams.

*(Solutions are on page 111)*

## Part 1

| | | |
|---|---|---|
| 1._____ | Joe Sakic | A. Oshawa Generals (OHL) |
| 2._____ | Keith Tkachuk | B. Sorel Eperviers (QMJHL) |
| 3._____ | Peter Bondra | C. University of Maine (HE) |
| 4._____ | Ray Bourque | D. CSKA (USSR) |
| 5._____ | Eric Lindros | E. Swift Current Broncos (WHL) |
| 6._____ | Mike Modano | F. Boston University (HE) |
| 7._____ | Paul Kariya | G. Prince Albert Raiders (WHL) |
| 8._____ | Pavel Bure | H. VSZ Kosice (Czech.) |

## Part 2

| | | |
|---|---|---|
| 1._____ | Brett Hull | A. Jokerit (Finland) |
| 2._____ | Mats Sundin | B. Niagara Falls Thunder (OHL) |
| 3._____ | Trevor Linden | C. Granby Bisons (QMJHL) |
| 4._____ | Pierre Turgeon | D. University of Vermont (ECAC) |
| 5._____ | Keith Primeau | E. Djurgarden (Sweden) |
| 6._____ | Teemu Selanne | F. London Knights (OHL) |
| 7._____ | John LeClair | G. Medicine Hat Tigers (WHL) |
| 8._____ | Brendan Shanahan | H. University of Minnesota-Duluth (WCHA) |

# 3

# THE ENVELOPE, PLEASE

Considering the long history of the Original Six teams, you would expect that a player from each of these clubs would have won the major NHL awards at least once. But that's not the case. The Norris Trophy, for best defenseman, has never been won by a player from one of the Original Six teams. Can you guess which team? Since the award's creation in 1954, the Toronto Maple Leafs have been blanked in the Norris balloting. Hopefully, you'll fare better than Toronto, as we step up to the podium and hand out the hardware.

*(Answers are on page 29)*

**3.1** Who was the first player to win the Hart Trophy as the NHL's most valuable player by a unanimous vote?
A. Maurice Richard
B. Gordie Howe
C. Bobby Orr
D. Wayne Gretzky

**3.2** The Hart Trophy was first awarded in 1924. How many years elapsed before an American-born player won the Hart?
A. One year
B. 18 years
C. 36 years
D. An American has never won it

**3.3** How many players have won the MVP Award, but not been elected to either the first or second NHL All-Star team?
A. One player
B. Two players
C. Three players
D. It has never happened

3.4 The Art Ross Trophy goes to the player who compiles the most points in a season. If players tie in points, the trophy goes to the one with the most goals. If the players also tie in goals, how is the winner determined?
A. It goes to the player who played the fewest games
B. It goes to the player who had the most multiple-goal games
C. It goes to the player who scored the most unassisted goals
D. It goes to the player who scored the most game-winning goals

3.5 As of 1996-97, Wayne Gretzky had won more Art Ross Trophies than any other player. How many scoring crowns has Gretzky won?
A. Six
B. Eight
C. 10
D. 12

3.6 When was the last time an Art Ross Trophy winner scored more goals than assists?
A. In the 1940s
B. In the 1950s
C. In the 1960s
D. In the 1970s

3.7 Who has won the most Vezina Trophies as the NHL's outstanding goaltender?
A. Ken Dryden
B. Terry Sawchuk
C. Jacques Plante
D. Bill Durnan

3.8 The Calder Trophy, honouring the NHL's top rookie, was named in honour of Frank Calder. Who was Frank Calder?
A. The first trustee of the Stanley Cup
B. The first president of the NHL
C. The first owner of the New York Rangers
D. The first referee-in-chief of the NHL

**3.9** Which player's selection as the NHL's rookie of the year prompted a rule change in the voting for the Calder Trophy?
A. Denis Potvin
B. Ken Dryden
C. Peter Stastny
D. Sergei Makarov

**3.10** Of the players who have won the Norris Trophy as the NHL's top defenseman since expansion in 1967-68, which blueliner claimed the award with the fewest points?
A. Bobby Orr
B. Chris Chelios
C. Rod Langway
D. Larry Robinson

**3.11** The original Lady Byng Trophy, honouring "sportsmanship, gentlemanly conduct and a high standard of playing ability," was given to which player to keep after he won the award seven times in eight years?
A. Syl Apps
B. Max Bentley
C. Frank Boucher
D. Howie Morenz

**3.12** What is the most penalty minutes ever collected by a winner of the Lady Byng Trophy?
A. 20
B. 40
C. 60
D. 80

**3.13** Who is the only player to win four major individual NHL awards in one season?
A. Bobby Orr
B. Stan Mikita
C. Ed Belfour
D. Wayne Gretzky

**3.14** The Frank Selke Trophy is awarded to the forward who best excels in the defensive aspects of the game. Who is the only four-time winner of the Selke?
A. Guy Carbonneau
B. Bob Gainey
C. Sergei Fedorov
D. Ron Francis

**3.15** Which award is presented annually to the player judged to be the NHL's most outstanding player, as selected by the players themselves?
A. The Lester Patrick Trophy
B. The King Clancy Memorial Trophy
C. The Lester B. Pearson Award
D. The William M. Jennings Trophy

# THE ENVELOPE, PLEASE
## *Answers*

**3.1** **D. Wayne Gretzky**
In 1981–82, Gretzky was unstoppable. The Great One set new NHL records for goals (92), assists (120) and points (212), and finished an eye-popping 65 points ahead of runner-up Mike Bossy in the scoring race. In recognition of his scoring exploits, the 63 voting members of the Professional Hockey Writers Association made Gretzky an unanimous choice for the Hart Trophy.

**3.2** **A. One year**
The Hart Trophy was awarded only once before an American nabbed it in 1925. The recipient was Billy Burch, who hailed from Yonkers, New York. At six foot and 200 pounds, Burch was a big man for his time and he had a big impact on the NHL, leading the New York Americans in scoring five times. But the year Burch won the Hart, he was the top point getter for the first-place Hamilton Tigers.

### 3.3 B. Two players

It's hard to imagine an MVP winner not being voted to either the first or second All-Star teams, but that's exactly what occurred in 1954 and 1955. Blackhawks goalie Al Rollins got the nod as MVP in 1954, despite playing for a last-place club and having the worst goals-against average in the league. However, the voters selected Harry Lumley and Terry Sawchuk as the All-Star goalies that year. Centre Ted Kennedy of the Maple Leafs earned MVP honours the next year, despite counting only 10 goals and finishing 11th in the scoring race. But Kennedy finished behind Jean Béliveau and Ken Mosdell in the All-Star balloting for his position.

### 3.4 A. It goes to the player who played the fewest games

This rule has yet to be tested. Though two players have tied for the scoring title on three occasions—Bobby Hull and Andy Bathgate in 1961-62, Marcel Dionne and Wayne Gretzky in 1979-80, and Jaromir Jagr and Eric Lindros in 1994-95—in each case the winner (Hull, Dionne and Jagr) was determined by most goals. If a situation should arise where two players are tied in points and goals, and they have also played the same number of games, then the third criterion will be used—the winner would be the player who scored earliest in the season.

### 3.5 C. 10

Of the dozens of scoring records that Gretzky owns, this may prove to be one of the most difficult to break. No. 99 has won 10 Art Ross Trophies as the NHL's top scorer, including seven in a row during the 1980s. From 1981 to 1994, the only player to break his stranglehold on the category was Mario Lemieux, who won the crown in 1988, 1989, 1992 and 1993. He also won it in 1996 and 1997.

### 3.6 C. In the 1960s

Bobby Hull was the last player to win an NHL scoring title with more goals than assists. Hull notched 54 goals and 43 assists for a league-high 97 points in 1965-66. Phil Esposito came within one goal of doing it in 1970-71, and was two goals shy in 1971-72.

### 3.7  C. Jacques Plante

Plante will always be remembered as the man who popularized the goalie mask, but he also left behind a legacy of other notable achievements, including his record seven Vezina Trophies. Plante collected the first six with Montreal between 1955-56 and 1961-62, equalling former Canadiens great Bill Durnan for the most in NHL history. Plante came out of retirement in 1968-69, and won his record-breaking seventh Vezina at age 40 with St. Louis. That season, he and 37-year-old Glenn Hall shared goaltending duties with the Blues and combined to record a league-high 13 shutouts and a sparkling 2.07 goals-against average.

### Jacques Plante's Vezina Trophy Tally

| Year | Team | GP | SO | GAA |
|------|------|-----|-----|------|
| 1955-56 | Montreal | 64 | 7 | 1.86 |
| 1956-57 | Montreal | 61 | 9 | 2.02 |
| 1957-58 | Montreal | 57 | 9 | 2.11 |
| 1958-59 | Montreal | 67 | 9 | 2.16 |
| 1959-60 | Montreal | 69 | 3 | 2.54 |
| 1961-62 | Montreal | 70 | 4 | 2.37 |
| 1968-69 | St. Louis | 37 | 5 | 1.96 |

### 3.8  B. The first president of the NHL

Frank Calder came to Canada from England in 1900, as a 23-year-old schoolteacher. He went on to become a crusading Montreal sportswriter, and was elected as the NHL's first president in 1917, a post he held until his death in 1943. From 1937 until 1943, Calder bought a trophy each year, to be presented to the NHL's outstanding rookie. After his death, the NHL created the Calder Memorial Trophy in his honour.

### 3.9  D. Sergei Makarov

Makarov won the Calder Trophy as the NHL's top rookie in 1989-90, when he counted 86 points with Calgary. But his election was a controversial one. Makarov was 31 years old, having joined the Flames after playing 11 seasons with the

Soviet Red Army Team. Many thought that his age and experience should have disqualified him from consideration as a rookie, and that the award should rightfully have gone to 20-year-old Mike Modano. In response to the criticism, the NHL changed its eligibility rules the next year. A player must now be under 26 years of age by September 15 of his rookie season to qualify for the Calder.

### 3.10  A.  Bobby Orr

Hockey's greatest offensive defenseman won the Norris Trophy with just 31 points in 1967-68, the lowest total of any D-man since expansion. Washington's Rod Langway is a close runner-up in the category, having won two Norris Trophies with 32 and 33 points respectively. Orr did have an excuse for his low point production—a knee injury sidelined him for 28 games during 1967-68. Still, in the 46 games he played, he impressed enough people to win the Norris, the first of eight straight that would end up on his mantelpiece. Actually, 31 points wasn't a bad total for a defenseman at the time. Orr soon changed that with his off-the-chart numbers, making the Norris almost exclusively the domain of defensemen who create goals rather than prevent them.

### 3.11  C.  Frank Boucher

The classy New York Ranger centre claimed the Lady Byng Trophy seven times in eight years between 1928 and 1935. After Boucher's seventh win, the NHL gave him the award to keep; a new Lady Byng Trophy was presented in 1936.

### 3.12  B.  40

The Lady Byng Trophy, awarded annually to the NHL player judged "to have exhibited the best type of sportsmanship and gentlemanly conduct, combined with a high standard of playing ability," was first presented in 1925. Winners usually have low penalty-minute totals. Only twice has the award gone to a player with 40 PIM—to Frank Nighbor of the Ottawa Senators in 1926 and to Billy Burch of the New York Americans in 1927. As the season was only 44 games at the time, those were fairly high penalty-minute totals, an indication that the standards of gentlemanly conduct have changed over the years.

### 3.13 A. Bobby Orr

"Bobby was a star from the moment they played the national anthem in his first NHL game," said Boston coach Harry Sinden. Few who had the pleasure of watching Orr in his prime would disagree. Orr's star never shone any brighter than in 1969-70, when the 22-year-old led the Bruins to the Stanley Cup and walked off with an unprecedented four major trophies. Orr won the Hart Trophy as league MVP, the Art Ross Trophy as top scorer, the Norris Trophy as top defenseman and the Conn Smythe Trophy as MVP of the playoffs.

### 3.14 B. Bob Gainey

Montreal fans asked "Bob who?" when the Canadiens used their first-round draft pick in 1973 to select Bob Gainey from the OHL's Peterborough Petes. Gainey had struggled to score even 22 goals in the junior ranks; how could he possibly add to the Habs' attack? But general manager Sam Pollock wasn't looking for a scorer. He wanted a frontline checker. Gainey filled that role to perfection, shutting down the opposition's top scoring threats and providing gritty team leadership for 16 years with Montreal. When the NHL created the Frank Selke Award to honour defensive play by a forward in 1978, it seemed tailor-made for Gainey. He won the first four Selkes, a total that no other player has matched.

### 3.15 C. The Lester B. Pearson Award

Many mistakenly believe that the Hart Trophy is awarded to the NHL's outstanding player. But the Hart, which is voted on by the media, goes to the player judged to be most valuable to his team. It is the Pearson, which is voted on by the players themselves, that honours individual excellence. First presented in 1971, the Pearson winners list reveals some interesting anomalies. For example, Bobby Orr, who won three Hart Trophies, earned only one Pearson; Wayne Gretzky, a nine-time Hart winner, has received only five Pearsons.

# GAME 3
# CROSSWORD

## Across

*(Solutions are on page 112)*

4. _____ Turnbull, Leaf D-man
5. Put your dukes _____
7. Jacques _____, mask pioneer
10. Michel _____, journeyman goalie
13. First word of 36 Across
15. Bobby _____, old Habs sniper
17. Neutral zone _____
18. Full name of Stars "C" traded to Devils
20. _____ Magnifique, Mario Lemieux
21. Garth _____, Flyers goalie
23. Brother of Phil Esposito
24. J. P. _____, 1970s Hawk
25. _____ Ranford
28. Colorado's Scott _____
29. "_____ Bad Bruins"
31. Score a _____
32. John _____, 1980s Wing/Ranger
35. Injured
36. Most famous hockey phrase

## Down

1. Full name of 1990s Devils/Senators/Bruins goalie
2. Full name of Oilers/Blues goalie
3. Montreal team
6. Defensive specialty unit
8. Igor _____
9. Ray _____, 1980s Whaler/Jet
11. Mike _____, 1980s Blues/Whalers/Caps goalie
12. Teemu _____
14. Jean _____, Habs "C"
19. Cam _____
22. Ken _____, Pens goalie
26. Isles Chris _____
27. Colorado's Rene _____
29. Craig _____, Caps journeyman,
30. Mickey _____, 1920s Hamilton Tiger
33. Spurt
34. He _____ the puck

34

# 4

# ICE OUTLAWS

It's not often that hockey-playing brothers rumble, so when the brothers Primeau duked it out during a 1997 Buffalo-Hartford game, it got noticed. Brother Wayne, 20, ran Hartford goalie Sean Burke, so brother Keith, 25, entered the fracas to defend his netminder. The brothers dropped their gloves and Keith won the decision after Wayne hit the ice first. "There was some hesitation," Keith said. "I knew who he was. That's blood, man." The elder Primeau was so upset, he called his parents between periods to apologize. Hartford coach Paul Maurice concluded: "It must have been pretty tough at the Primeau dinner table when there was only one pork chop left."

Blood sport, or not, in this round we go toe-to-toe with hockey's heavyweight legends. Put 'em up.

*(Answers are on page 39)*

**4.1** Which former NHL enforcer fought an exhibition bout with heavyweight champion Muhammad Ali?
A. Dave Schultz
B. Tiger Williams
C. John Ferguson
D. Dave Semenko

**4.2** Who is the only NHLer to rank in the top 10 scorers and collect more than 250 minutes in penalties in the same season?
A. Al Secord
B. Brendan Shanahan
C. Kevin Stevens
D. Rick Tocchet

**4.3** Which player did Buffalo Sabres enforcer Rob Ray say he wanted to hurt the most?

A. Tie Domi

B. Tony Twist

C. Ulf Samuelsson

D. Bryan Marchment

**4.4** What new piece of NHL legislation was dubbed the "Rob Ray rule"?

A. Any player who head-butts an opponent receives a game misconduct

B. Any player engaging in a fight off the playing surface receives a game misconduct

C. Any player who removes his jersey before or during a fight receives a game misconduct

D. Any player who deliberately knees an opponent receives a match penalty

**4.5** Which Detroit player beat up Colorado's Claude Lemieux in 1997, to avenge the vicious hit from behind Lemieux had laid on Red Wing Kris Draper during the 1996 playoffs?

A. Brendan Shanahan

B. Darren McCarty

C. Martin Lapointe

D. Jamie Pushor

**4.6** In 1996, a Canadian rock band called the Hanson Brothers launched a campaign to get which former hockey tough guy elected to the Hockey Hall of Fame?

A. Eddie Shack

B. Terry O'Reilly

C. John Ferguson

D. Tiger Williams

**4.7** Who was the first NHLer to rack up more than 200 penalty minutes in a season?

A. Detroit's Howie Young

B. Montreal's John Ferguson

C. New York's Lou Fontinato

D. Chicago's Reggie Fleming

**4.8** What is the professional hockey record for most penalty minutes in a season?
A. 448
B. 548
C. 648
D. 748

**4.9** Which old-time hockey roughneck was nicknamed "Scarface"?
A. Detroit's Ted Lindsay
B. Boston's Eddie Shore
C. Toronto's Red Horner
D. Detroit's Jimmy Orlando

**4.10** Who is the most penalized player in Philadelphia Flyers franchise history?
A. Paul Holmgren
B. Rick Tocchet
C. Dave Schultz
D. Bobby Clarke

**4.11** After duking it out a couple of times with Marty McSorley in 1996-97, which NHL brawler took a few more potshots at McSorley in the press, accusing him of being a cheap-shot artist?
A. Vancouver's Gino Odjick
B. Calgary's Sandy McCarthy
C. Washington's Chris Simon
D. Chicago's Jim Cummins

**4.12** Which former NHL brawler died after a violent struggle with police officers in 1992?
A. Randy Holt
B. John Kordic
C. Stan Jonathan
D. Steve Durbano

**4.13** What is the record for most penalty minutes in a season by a goaltender?

A. 44
B. 74
C. 104
D. 134

**4.14** Which old-time hockey hooligan boasted that he had been involved in 50 "stretcher-case fights" during his career?

A. Red Horner
B. Eddie Shore
C. Sprague Cleghorn
D. Black Jack Stewart

**4.15** Which Calgary player scaled the glass partition behind the Flames bench in Edmonton on November 23, 1997, to get at a heckling fan?

A. Sasha Lakovic
B. Todd Simpson
C. Ron Stern
D. Cal Hulse

**4.16** Which coach was hit with the largest fine in NHL history for attacking a referee?

A. Montreal's Toe Blake
B. Boston's Don Cherry
C. New York's Red Sullivan
D. Chicago's Billy Reay

## ICE OUTLAWS
### *Answers*

**4.1** **D. Dave Semenko**

Semenko climbed into the ring with Ali to fight a three-round exhibition in Edmonton in the eighties. Semenko trained seriously for the bout. Too seriously, in fact. As he recalls in his book, *Looking Out for Number One*, during one training session a member of Ali's entourage came over to Semenko and said, "Listen, make sure you don't do something stupid like trying to take the champ's head off." Semenko got the message. Neither he nor Ali landed any serious blows during the bout.

### 4.2  C. Kevin Stevens

Before Stevens's injury in the 1994 playoffs, he was that rare NHL commodity—a big-time gunner with a serious mean streak. In 1991-92, Stevens scored 123 points (54 goals and 69 assists) with Pittsburgh to finish second in the scoring race, behind linemate Mario Lemieux. He also compiled 254 penalty minutes, the highest total by a top 10 scorer in NHL history.

### 4.3  A. Tie Domi

Ray pulled no punches in expressing his feelings about Domi. "I hate his guts. There's nobody else in the league I feel that way about. I just love pounding on his big head." Ray went on to say, "In all the years I played here in Buffalo, there were only two guys I couldn't stand: Christian Ruutu and that little puke Phil Housley. But even slapping them around wouldn't give me the satisfaction of laying a beating on Domi."

### 4.4  C. Any player who removes his sweater during a fight receives a game misconduct

The Sabres' Rob Ray was the player chiefly responsible for the NHL rule that penalizes a player for shucking his jersey before or during a scrap. Ray liked to wear a loose jersey, with his protective equipment sewn onto it so he could easily pull it off and fire punches without any restraints. (Also, Ray never wore a T-shirt; that way, his opponent had nothing to grab onto to tie him up.) The technique may have helped him get the upper hand in his fights, but the repeated appearances of Ray's naked torso on the highlight reels was not an image the NHL wanted to project, so it amended its rule.

### 4.5  B. Darren McCarty

The March 26, 1997, match was the first time Lemieux had played in Detroit since the 1996 playoff incident, and by

McCarty's accounting it was a great game—"like old-time hockey." The press dubbed the bloodletting the "Brawl in Hockeytown," and continued replaying its highlights for days afterwards. The fight began in retaliation for Lemieux's nasty backside cross-check on Draper during game six of 1996's Western Conference final. Lemieux got a two-game suspension, but Draper sustained multiple fractures and required major facial and oral surgery. Fast forward to Lemieux's next meeting with Detroit, 10 months later. With two minutes left in the first period, Igor Larionov and Peter Forsberg collided along the boards. No big deal. But in the ensuing scuffle, McCarty took revenge and sucker-punched Lemieux to the ice. Lemieux turtled while McCarty continued pummelling away. Patrick Roy stormed out of his crease to help Lemieux, but Brendan Shanahan intercepted Roy with a heavy check at centre ice. That caused Wing backstopper Mike Vernon to enter the fray, and the two goalies slugged it out toe-to-toe, with Vernon winning the bout. After 60 minutes of bloody hockey, 18 fighting majors and 148 penalty minutes, the game went into overtime tied 5-5. Who scored the winner? On a nice offensive move, Shanahan pulled Roy to the right side of the goal and passed to McCarty, who fired home the tie breaker. McCarty settled a couple of scores that night. Draper said he felt "a sense of closure" after the fight-filled game, and Detroit's 6-5 win was their first after three consecutive losses to Colorado, along with the series loss in the 1966 Western Conference final.

## 4.6   D. Tiger Williams

Rock music's Hanson Brothers (who are not related to the Hanson brothers of *Slapshot* fame) kick-started their crusade to get Williams into the Hockey Hall of Fame at the October 1996 launch of their CD, *Sudden Death*. The album features 15 songs about girls, beer and hockey, including "Stick Boy," "Third Man In," "Rink Rat" and a tune called "He Looked a Lot Like Tiger Williams," in which the NHL's all-time penalty leader is likened to a doctor, a traffic cop and God. Included with each CD was a ballot, which the Hansons asked people to sign and return, boosting Williams for the Hall ahead of "some of those fancy-schmancy no-hitting prima donna whining millionaire goal sucks." In response to the campaign, Williams said he doubts he will ever make it into the Hall, but if he does he knows the ideal spot. "I should be in the refs' section, because I made their lives interesting. The only time they got their mugs on TV was when they were in the middle of a fight wiping my blood off their faces."

**4.7   C. New York's Lou Fontinato**

During the 1950s, Leapin' Lou enjoyed a reputation as the NHL's resident bad boy and premier pugilist. In 1955-56, the Ranger defenseman compiled 202 penalty minutes in 70 games to break Red Horner's record of 167 PIM, set in the 1935-36 48-game schedule. However, in February 1959, Fontinato made the mistake of challenging Gordie Howe. The big Red Wing shook off Fontinato's initial flurry of punches, grabbed the neck of his tormentor's jersey, and began repeatedly driving his right hand into Fontinato's face. By the time Howe was done, Leapin' Lou's nose and cheekbone were mashed to a bloody pulp; plastic surgeons had to rearrange his face. The thumping ruined Fontinato. Some say it did the same to the Rangers, who slumped badly in the last half of the season, eventually missing the playoffs by one point.

**4.8   C. 648**

At five foot nine and 185 pounds, Kevin Evans was no heavyweight, but he put up some heavyweight penalty numbers. In 1986-87, the rookie winger racked up 648 minutes of box time in 73 games with the Kalamazoo Wings of the IHL. It still stands as a professional hockey record. Evans later had a brief pitstop in the NHL. He played four games with Minnesota in 1990-91 and five games with San Jose in 1991-92, recording no goals, one assist and 44 penalty minutes.

**4.9   A. Detroit's Ted Lindsay**

Despite his small size (five foot eight and 160 pounds), Lindsay was a fearless player who battled all comers with his stick and his fists. Blood often ran freely when Terrible Ted was on the ice, including his own. Lindsay stopped counting his stitches after they reached 200, but there was no ignoring the toll on his facial features. Former NHL referee Red Storey described Lindsay as having "one of those faces that holds about three days of rain." Opposition players were less poetic. They called him Scarface.

### 4.10  B.  Rick Tocchet

Somewhat surprisingly, Tocchet accumulated more penalty minutes as a Flyer than any of the hell-raisers from the club's infamous Broad Street Bully days. The hard-nosed winger collected 1,683 PIM in 531 games in Philly. Dave "The Hammer" Schultz, the player who you might expect to own this record, ranks fourth on the Flyers' all-time penalty chart. Schultz spent only five years with the Flyers before taking his Attila the Hun act to Los Angeles. Another season of mayhem in the City of Brotherly Love would have elevated Schultz to the top of the chart.

### The Flyers' All-Time Bad Boys*

| Player | Years | GP | PIM |
|---|---|---|---|
| Rick Tocchet | 1982-1992 | 531 | 1,683 |
| Paul Holmgren | 1975-1984 | 500 | 1,600 |
| Andre Dupont | 1972-1980 | 549 | 1,505 |
| Bobby Clarke | 1969-1984 | 1,144 | 1,453 |
| Dave Schultz | 1972-1976 | 297 | 1,386 |
| Dave Brown | 1982-1988 | 552 | 1,382 |

*Current to 1997*

### 4.11  B.  Calgary's Sandy McCarthy

McCarthy made it clear that he does not belong to the Marty McSorley fan club. "Let's just say I have a grudge against him and a score to settle," said McCarthy. "He's a big man, a strong man and a respected fighter. But he's also a jerk who hands out a lot of cheap shots. He's always cutting guys from behind or giving them cheap shots. There's a code involved here and sometimes McSorley forgets that. He's one of the worst. I respect the guy as a fighter, but I wouldn't trust him."

## 4.12 B. John Kordic

Kordic's last fight was fatal. On August 8, 1992, police were called to a Quebec City motel, where the former enforcer was living, after hotel staff complained of abusive behaviour and a loud disturbance in his room. The police officers who responded to the call found Kordic extremely agitated and intoxicated. When they tried to take him to the hospital for treatment, he resisted, throwing punches and screaming. It eventually took nine officers to subdue him. Shortly after the ambulance left the motel, Kordic passed out. He could not be revived. An autopsy showed that he died from heart failure, the result of mixing alcohol, cocaine and steroids. He was only 27.

## 4.13 C. 104

Rookie Ron Hextall made a striking impression with the Philadelphia Flyers in 1986-87, combining acrobatic puckstopping with a tomahawk stick hand. When he wasn't using his goal stick to let fly breakout passes, he was hacking and chopping at opposing players who wandered into his crease. The hotheaded Hextall won the Vezina Trophy as top netminder and also logged 104 penalty minutes, a record for goalies.

## 4.14 C. Sprague Cleghorn

Many old-timers insist that Cleghorn was the nastiest customer to ever lace on a pair of skates. During his 18-year career, he carved out a notorious reputation. Jack Adams, who played against Cleghorn, called him "an unwashed surgeon." In one game alone in 1921, Cleghorn disabled three Ottawa Senator players. After the game, the Ottawa police offered to arrest him for assault. During the 1923 playoffs, Cleghorn stick-whipped Lionel Hitchman of the Ottawa Senators so severely that Cleghorn's own manager, Leo Dandurand of the Canadiens, fined him $200 and suspended him. Before he died in 1953, Cleghorn boasted, "All told, I figure I was in 50 stretcher-case fights. I didn't lose any."

### 4.15 A. Sasha Lakovic

In a spectacle reminiscent of the famous glass-climbing incident involving three Boston players at Madison Square Garden in the 1970s, Lakovic scaled the glass partition behind Calgary's bench at Edmonton's Northlands Coliseum in an attempt to reach a heckler, who had dumped rum and coke and a bag of popcorn over the head of Flames assistant coach Guy Lapointe. Lakovic failed, but Lapointe, from a better position atop the glass, appeared to land a hard right. Lakovic received a $1,000 fine and two-game suspension. The drunken heckler, Raymond Howarth, 27, of Whitecourt, Alberta, pleaded guilty to mischief and was handed a 30-day jail sentence and fined $1,000. Howarth's lawyer called his client's action "an act of childish stupidity."

### 4.16 A. Montreal's Toe Blake

Referee Dalton MacArthur drew Blake's ire during the third game of the 1961 semifinals in Chicago by disallowing two Montreal goals. When the Hawks' Murray Balfour finally won the game on a power-play tally in the third overtime period, a red-faced Blake rushed on the ice and threw a roundhouse right at MacArthur. Blake claimed the punch hadn't landed, but the league thought otherwise and fined him $2,000, a fortune in those days. The headline in the next day's paper read: "Toe Gets $2,000 Sock."

# GAME 4

# PENALTY LEADERS

Listed below are many of the NHL's most feared players. These bad boys appear in the puzzle horizontally, vertically, diagonally or backwards. After you've circled all 46 words or names (like N-I-L-A-N), read the remaining letters in descending order to spell the name of the tough guy who led the league in penalty minutes most often.

*(Solutions are on page 113)*

| | | | | | |
|---|---|---|---|---|---|
| BARILKO | BARNABY | BAXTER | BENCH | BOUCHER | BREWER |
| CICCONE | CLEGHORN | CLIP | CORBEAU | DOMI | DURBANO |
| DUTTON | EGAN | EZINICKI | FERGUSON | FIGHTS | FLAMAN |
| FONTINATO | GOALS | HADFIELD | HALL | HOLT | HUNTER |
| KOCUR | KYLE | LINDSAY | MAGNUSON | MANN | MCMAHON |
| MCRAE | MCSORLEY | MORTSON | NILAN | ORLANDO | PELUSO |
| PILOTE | RICHARD | RULES | SCHULTZ | SHORE | STEWART |
| TRIP | WATSON | WILLIAMS | YOUNG | | |

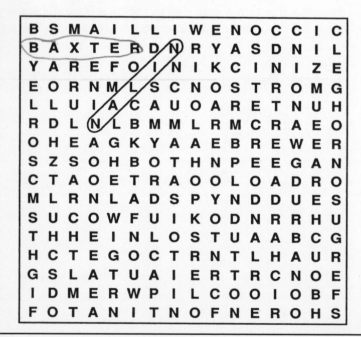

```
B S M A I L L I W E N O C C I C
B A X T E R D N R Y A S D N I L
Y A R E F O I N I K C I N I Z E
E O R N M L S C N O S T R O M G
L L U I A C A U O A R E T N U H
R D L N L B M M L R M C R A E O
O H E A G K Y A A E B R E W E R
S Z S O H B O T H N P E E G A N
C T A O E T R A O O L O A D R O
M L R N L A D S P Y N D D U E S
S U C O W F U I K O D N R R H U
T H H E I N L O S T U A A B C G
H C T E G O C T R N T L H A U R
G S L A T U A I E R T R C N O E
I D M E R W P I L C O O I O B F
F O T A N I T N O F N E R O H S
```

# 5

# ONLY THE LONELY

In his rookie season, Patrick Roy attracted media attention with his eccentric habit of skating out to the blueline before a game and communicating telepathically with his goalposts. "I talk to my posts," he admitted. "It's a superstition. The forwards talk to each other. The defense is always close, but the goaltender is alone."

Roy has a point. Goalies are isolated on the ice, both by their position and by their attitude. Only a goalie can virtually win a game by himself—or lose one. It takes a special mentality to cope with that type of intense pressure. When things go wrong there's no lonelier spot on the ice.

*(Answers are on page 51)*

**5.1** Which goalie was Ron Hextall talking about when he said: "It's hard to beat this guy. This guy doesn't know what he's going to do."?
A. Mike Richter
B. Dominik Hasek
C. Martin Brodeur
D. Hextall was talking about himself

**5.2** Which NHL goalie registered the first double-digit shutout season since Ken Dryden posted 10 shutouts in 1976-77?
A. Colorado's Patrick Roy
B. Phoenix's Nikolai Khabibulin
C. Detroit's Chris Osgood
D. New Jersey's Martin Brodeur

5.3 If Buffalo's Dominik Hasek played in 67 games (4,037 minutes) in 1996-97 and faced 2,177 shots, how many shots did Martin Brodeur face in his 67 games (3,838 minutes) for the New Jersey Devils—the most successful team to employ the neutral-zone trap?
A. Less than 1,777
B. Between 1,777 and 1,977
C. Between 1,977 and 2,177
D. Exactly the same, 2,177

5.4 What is the greatest number of shots an NHL netminder has faced in a season?
A. Between 1,700 and 1,900
B. Between 1,900 and 2,100
C. Between 2,100 and 2,300
D. Between 2,300 and 2,500

5.5 Who is the only goalie to hold the single-season shutout record for both an Original Six team and an expansion club?
A. Terry Sawchuk
B. Glenn Hall
C. Pete Peeters
D. Gump Worsley

5.6 What do goalies Curtis Joseph and Ed Belfour have in common?
A. Both were born on the same day
B. Both were voted IHL rookie of the year
C. Both had shutouts in their first NHL game
D. Neither was drafted by an NHL team

5.7 Which NHL goaltender was born in South Africa?
A. Damian Rhodes
B. Olaf Kolzig
C. Daren Puppa
D. Corey Hirsch

5.8 When Vancouver's Mike Fountain recorded a 3-0 shutout in his NHL debut in November 1996, it was *not* a league first. How many netminders before Fountain posted shutouts in their first NHL start?
A. Less than five
B. Between six and 10
C. Between 11 and 15
D. More than 16

5.9 Rookie netminder Patrick Lalime of the Pittsburgh Penguins set an NHL record for most consecutive undefeated games at the start of a career, by going undefeated in how many games in 1996-97?
A. 10
B. 13
C. 16
D. 19

5.10 From which team did the Florida Panthers claim John Vanbiesbrouck in the 1994 expansion draft?
A. The Vancouver Canucks
B. The Washington Capitals
C. The New York Rangers
D. The Calgary Flames

5.11 Which team chased Patrick Roy from the net by scoring nine goals on him in his last game for the Montreal Canadiens, December 2, 1995?
A. The Pittsburgh Penguins
B. The New York Rangers
C. The Detroit Red Wings
D. The Philadelphia Flyers

5.12 Who is the only goalie to record three straight shutouts in a playoff series?
A. "Mr. Zero," Frank Brimsek
B. "The Shutout King," Terry Sawchuk
C. "Tony O," Tony Esposito
D. Frank "Ulcers" McCool

**5.13 What is the maximum width allowed for a goalie's leg pads?**
A. Eight inches
B. 10 inches
C. 12 inches
D. 14 inches

**5.14 What is goalie Lorne Chabot's claim to fame?**
A. He was the first ex-goalie to coach a Stanley Cup champion
B. He played two seasons as an NHL defenseman
C. He tended goal for the two longest games in NHL history
D. He holds the NHL mark for most consecutive shutouts in a season

**5.15 Who is the only NHL netminder to register 30 or more wins in seven consecutive seasons?**
A. Grant Fuhr
B. Ken Dryden
C. Jacques Plante
D. Tony Esposito

**5.16 Who is the only NHL goalie to post a goals-against average of under 2.00 in five straight seasons?**
A. Ken Dryden
B. Turk Broda
C. Jacques Plante
D. Terry Sawchuk

**5.17 Which NHL goalie's mask bears the image of a snarling animal that was featured in a horror film?**
A. The Oiler's Curtis Joseph
B. The Devils' Martin Brodeur
C. The Kings' Stephane Fiset
D. The Panthers' John Vanbiesbrouck

# ONLY THE LONELY
## *Answers*

**5.1  B.  Dominik Hasek**
The Sabres netminder mesmerized opposition shooters (and apparently Hextall) with his unorthodox style in 1996-97. Hextall's quote about Hasek came after a frustrating 3-2 Flyers loss to the Sabres on March 11, 1997. "It's hard to tell how to beat this guy. This guy doesn't know what he's going to do. So, therefore, neither does the shooter. He has no pattern to the way he stops the puck. A guy on a breakaway has no clue what Hasek will do. Most goalies stick to a style. Not this guy. He's on his back, he's flipping over. You have to shoot high on him. He covers low very well."

**5.2  D.  New Jersey's Martin Brodeur**
Twenty years after Ken Dryden recorded the NHL's last double-digit shutout season, Brodeur equalled that mark with his league-leading 10 SOs in 1996-97. Not to deny Brodeur his due as one of hockey's best goalies (he was 1994's rookie of the year), his achievement is due in part to the Devils' neutral-zone trap. (Designed to stall opponents at the centre redline, the trap floods the neutral zone with players to force a turnover.) The trap's greatest success has come in New Jersey, where Brodeur earned another accolade in 1996-97. The Devils goalie had a goals-against average of 1.88, the best in the league since Tony Esposito's 1.77 in 48 games in 1971-72.

**5.3  A.  Less than 1,777**
Despite playing an identical number of games (with different total minutes played) and registering 37 wins each, Brodeur faced far fewer shots than his Buffalo rival, Hasek. While Hasek faced 2,177 shots in 1996-97, Brodeur's season total was 25 per cent less, only 1,633 shots. If there ever was a statistic that proved the effectiveness of the trap, this might be it.

**5.4  D.  Between 2,300 and 2,500**
In 1993-94, Curtis Joseph, backstopping St. Louis' porous

defense corps, faced an amazing 2,382 shots in 71 games. Incredibly, that rubber mark was passed in 1996-97 by shell-shocked Felix Potvin, who played 74 games for the 23rd-place Toronto Maple Leafs, allowing 224 goals on 2,438 shots.

## 5.5  B.  Glenn Hall

Hall shares the single-season shutout record for Detroit and owns the St. Louis record outright. His 12 shutouts in 1955-56 with Detroit equalled the mark set by Terry Sawchuk, who logged 12 SOs for the Wings three times: in 1951-52, 1953-54 and 1954-55. The eight goose eggs Hall recorded in 1968-69 with St. Louis remains a franchise high. However, Hall does not own the single-season shutout mark for Chicago, the team with which he spent most of his career. That honour belongs to Tony Esposito, who posted 15 shutouts with the Hawks in 1969-70.

## 5.6  D.  Neither was drafted by an NHL team

The scouts don't always get it right, especially with goalies. Curtis Joseph and Ed Belfour are prime examples. Neither was selected in the NHL Entry Draft, but both were quickly signed as free agents: Joseph, a 1989 All-Star at the University of Wisconsin, inked with St. Louis in June 1989; Belfour, a 1987 All-Star at the University of North Dakota, signed with Chicago in September 1987.

## 5.7  B.  Olaf Kolzig

Although Kolzig was raised in Canada, he was actually born in Johannesburg, South Africa. Kolzig's parents are both German. His father was a nuclear physicist who escaped from East Germany in 1958. After he married Olaf's mother, the pair moved to South Africa, where Kolzig was born in 1970. Kolzig has retained his German citizenship, which enabled him to play for the German national hockey team at the 1996 World Cup.

## 5.8  D.  More than 16

With both regular Canuck goalies on the sidelines—Kirk McLean with a knee injury and Corey Hirsch with the flu—Fountain was called up from the minors to make his NHL debut on November 14, 1996, versus the New Jersey Devils. Fountain responded by making 40 saves to blank New Jersey 3-0. In doing so, he became the 19th netminder in history to post a shutout in his first NHL start, and the first in more than 11 years to manage the feat. Yet Fountain nearly accomplished something even more remarkable when he narrowly missed scoring into the Devils' empty net. His rink-long shot just slid by the post.

### The NHL's All-Time Rookie Shutout Starts*

| Goalie | Team | Date | Results | |
|--------|------|------|---------|---|
| Hal Winkler | NYR | 11/18/26 | MtlM 0 | at NYR 1 |
| Lorne Chabot | NYR | 11/27/26 | NYR 2 | at Mtl 0 |
| Tiny Thompson | Bos | 11/15/28 | Bos 1 | at Pit 0 |
| Alfie Moore | NYA | 01/30/37 | NYA 4 | at Mtl 0 |
| Earl Robertson | NYA | 11/04/37 | NYA 3 | at Chi 0 |
| Gord Henry | Bos | 01/23/49 | Mtl 0 | at Bos 3 |
| Dave Gatherum | Det | 10/11/53 | Tor 0 | at Det 3 |
| Robert Perreault | Mtl | 12/17/55 | Chi 0 | at Mtl 5 |
| Claude Pronovost | Bos | 01/14/56 | Bos 2 | at Mtl 0 |
| Marcel Paille | NYR | 11/02/57 | Bos 0 | at NYR 5 |
| Charlie Hodge | Mtl | 10/13/64 | Mtl 3 | at NYR 0 |
| Andre Gill | Bos | 12/23/67 | Bos 4 | at NYR 0 |
| Wayne Thomas | Mtl | 01/14/73 | Mtl 3 | at Van 0 |
| Gary Simmons | Cal | 10/11/74 | Atl 0 | at Cal 3 |
| Mario Lessard | LA | 10/26/78 | Buf 0 | at LA 6 |
| Robbie Moore | Phi | 03/06/79 | Col 0 | at Phi 5 |
| Mario Gosselin | Que | 02/26/84 | StL 0 | at Que 5 |
| Daren Puppa | Buf | 01/11/85 | Buf 2 | at Edm 0 |
| Mike Fountain | Van | 11/14/96 | Van 3 | at NJ 0 |

*Current to 1997

### 5.9   C. 16

Patrick Lalime's emergence as the main man in the Penguins net was as unexpected as it was sudden. The last goalie selected in the 1993 draft, and the 156th player taken overall, Lalime had spent two very ordinary seasons in the minors before being promoted to the big club early in 1996-97, as a backup to Ken

Wregget. When Wregget went down with a pulled hamstring, 22-year-old Lalime stepped into the breach and immediately went on a spectacular roll, going unbeaten in 16 straight games (14-0-2). His streak broke the NHL record of 14 games, shared by Montreal's Ken Dryden (12-0-2 in 1970-71) and Boston's Ross Brooks (11-0-3 in 1972-73). Colorado finally snapped the string by defeating Lalime and the Penguins 4-3 in overtime. Ironically, Lalime's goaltending opponent that night was none other than his idol, Patrick Roy.

### 5.10  A.  The Vancouver Canucks

Many have forgotten that Vancouver acquired John Vanbiesbrouck from the Rangers in exchange for Doug Lidster shortly before the 1994 expansion draft, but Pat Quinn undoubtedly remembers. The Canucks' general manager took Vanbiesbrouck for the sole purpose of leaving him unprotected in the expansion draft. The reason? Quinn wanted to keep backup netminder Kay Whitmore out of the clutches of the expansion Anaheim Mighty Ducks and Florida Panthers. The Panthers, of course, chose the Beezer with their first pick. Whitmore remained in Vancouver, where he would play only 11 more games before being traded to the Rangers. In retrospect, Quinn would have been better advised to keep Vanbiesbrouck and expose Kirk McLean to the draft. But McLean, who had just come off a sensational playoffs, was considered an untouchable, a description the Panthers now apply to Vanbiesbrouck.

### 5.11  C.  The Detroit Red Wings

Big-league pressures mean even the best have a bad night. But on December 2, 1995, when Detroit's scoring machine rolled into Montreal, Patrick Roy's bad night assumed profound importance—both for his career and the Canadiens. The Red Wings chased Roy from the net just 31:57 into the game, scoring nine goals on 26 shots. After the seventh goal, Sergei Fedorov took a long slapper, which Roy handled easily. Disgruntled Forum fans responded with mock applause. Roy raised both arms high in a kind of one-finger salute to the sellout crowd. Two goals later he was finally yanked by rookie coach

Mario Tremblay. Roy skated off the ice embarrassed and angry. Unbeknowst to anyone at the time, it was his last appearance for Montreal. As Roy walked behind the player's bench to the backup goalie's stool, he stopped in midstride beyond Tremblay, wheeled around and took several steps back behind the bench to the box seat of Canadiens president Ronald Corey. Roy pressed up against Corey and snorted, "This is my last game for Montreal." Roy then pushed past a glaring Tremblay, sat on the stool, cocked his head back and said, "Did you understand?" Roy, an icon of the game and the Habs' most popular player, was through in Montreal. Four days later, he was traded to Colorado, where he would help the Avalanche win the 1996 Stanley Cup. Ironically, the Avalanche defeated the Red Wings in the Western Conference finals, the team whose shelling had prompted Roy's trade from Montreal.

### 5.12  D. Frank "Ulcers" McCool

McCool, a rookie netminder who drank from a bottle of milk between periods to calm his inflamed ulcers, was the key performer in the Leafs' amazing march to the Cup in 1945. His stellar goaltending helped the Leafs upset Montreal in the semifinals, and he continued his heroics in the finals versus Detroit. McCool held the Wings off the scoresheet for a span of 188 minutes and 35 seconds as the Leafs blanked Detroit in the first three games, 1-0, 2-0 and 1-0. His streak ended midway through the first period of game four when Bill "Flash" Hollett scored for Detroit. The Wings went on to win 5-3 and followed up with victories in games five and six to knot the series at three games apiece. In the tension-racked seventh game, McCool's stomach pain grew so severe he left the ice with the score tied 1-1 in the third period. But after a 10-minute break of sipping milk in the dressing room, he returned to play. Shortly afterwards, Babe Pratt scored to put the Leafs up 2-1 and, with McCool gallantly holding the fort, Toronto hung on to take the Cup. It was McCool's only championship. He played just one more NHL season before his stomach problems forced him to retire.

### 5.13 C. 12 inches

In response to persistent complaints about goaltenders using illegal equipment, the NHL initiated a crackdown in 1996-97, enforcing size limits on blockers, catching mitts and leg pads. According to NHL Rule 21, each leg pad can't be wider than 12 inches—the dimensions allowed by *The Official Rules of the NHL* since 1989. Any goalie caught using illegal equipment gets a one-game suspension. This may not sound like a deterrent, but considering today's salaries, it could mean a major hit in the pocketbook. Patrick Roy, for example, who earns $4.5 million annually, would receive a fine of $55,000. The crackdown has had equipment manufacturers and specialists in fits, but, so far, no goalie has been suspended for oversize gear.

### 5.14 C. He tended goal for the two longest games in NHL history

Lorne Chabot, whose 11-year NHL career included stints with six teams, has the unique distinction of playing in the two longest games in NHL history (he won one and lost the other). Both games occurred in a separate semifinal playoff series: On April 9, 1933, Chabot was tending net for Toronto when they defeated Boston 1-0 in a classic 164-minute marathon; three years later, on March 24, 1936, Chabot was on the losing side, as his Maroons were beaten 1-0 by Detroit after 176 minutes of play.

### 5.15 D. Tony Esposito

Esposito's habit of playing far back in his crease and using a flopping butterfly style ran contrary to the rules of classic stand-up goaltending, but no one could quarrel with the results. From 1969-70 to 1975-76, the Chicago netminder performed with sustained brilliance, compiling seven straight seasons of 30 wins or more, to break Jacques Plante's record of six.

### 5.16 D. Terry Sawchuk

No netminder has taken the NHL by storm the way Sawchuk did in his first five full years. He earned All-Star berths in all five campaigns and won three Vezinas as the goalie allowing the fewest goals, being edged out by a single goal in the other two.

But perhaps the best measure of Sawchuk's excellence was his goals-against averages in those five fabulous seasons: 1.99, 1.90, 1.90, 1.94 and 1.96.

## Sawchuk's Fabulous Five Seasons

| Year | GP | MIN | SO | GAA |
|------|------|------|------|------|
| 1950-51 | 70 | 4200 | 11 | 1.99 |
| 1951-52 | 70 | 4200 | 12 | 1.90 |
| 1952-53 | 63 | 3780 | 9 | 1.90 |
| 1953-54 | 67 | 4000 | 12 | 1.94 |
| 1954-55 | 68 | 4040 | 12 | 1.96 |

## 5.17 A. The Oilers' Curtis Joseph

The image of a rabid St. Bernard is emblazoned on Joseph's mask. The dog was featured in the Steven King horror film *Cujo*. Of course, Cujo also happens to be Joseph's nickname. Artist Frank Cipra did the design. To balance the bloodthirsty image, Joseph had the initials MTT painted on the rear skull pad. MTT are the initials of his three children: Madison, Taylor and Tristan.

# GAME 5

# CHICO, GUMP AND JAKE THE SNAKE

Nicknames have always been a part of hockey. Their origins come from the press box and the fans, but most often, the dressing room provides the best resource for a player's moniker. It's here where practical jokes and personal habits inspire nicknames which become so popular that, in some cases, players are better known by their noms de hockey than their given names.

The puckstopping fraternity has its own tradition of imaginative monikers. "Gump," "Chico" and "Rogie" are more common than those players' real names. But who are "Red Light," "The Shutout King" and "Fast Eddie"? Some of the game's most celebrated nicknames belong to those who play between the pipes. In this game, match the real names of these goalies with their nicknames.

*(Solutions are on page 114)*

## Part 1

| | | | |
|---|---|---|---|
| 1. _____ | Dominik Hasek | A. | "The Cat" |
| 2. _____ | Glenn Hall | B. | "Chico" |
| 3. _____ | Chuck Rayner | C. | "The Dominator" |
| 4. _____ | Andre Racicot | D. | "The Chicoutimi Cucumber" |
| 5. _____ | Terry Sawchuk | E. | "Bonnie Prince Charlie" |
| 6. _____ | Georges Vezina | F. | "Red Light" |
| 7. _____ | Felix Potvin | G. | "Mr. Goalie" |
| 8. _____ | Glenn Resch | H. | "The Shutout King" |

## Part 2

1. _____ Patrick Roy     A. "Suitcase"
2. _____ Billy Smith     B. "St. Patrick"
3. _____ Cecil Thompson     C. "Turk"
4. _____ Tony Esposito     D. "Bunny"
5. _____ Michel Larocque     E. "Tiny"
6. _____ Walter Broda     F. "The Hatchet Man"
7. _____ Grant Fuhr     G. "Tony O"
8. _____ Gary Smith     H. "Cocoa"

## Part 3

1. _____ John Vanbiesbrouck     A. "Gump"
2. _____ Gerry Cheevers     B. "Mr. Zero"
3. _____ Jacques Plante     C. "Cheesey"
4. _____ Frank Brimsek     D. "Beezer"
5. _____ Steve Buzinski     E. "China Wall"
6. _____ Lorne Worsley     F. "King Richard"
7. _____ Richard Brodeur     G. "Puckgoesinski"
8. _____ Johnny Bower     H. "Jake the Snake"

## Part 4

1. _____ Ed Giacomin     A. "Ulcers"
2. _____ Emile Francis     B. "The Thinker"
3. _____ Jim Henry     C. "Rogie"
4. _____ Rogatien Vachon     D. "Apple Cheeks"
5. _____ Harry Lumley     E. "Fast Eddie"
6. _____ Roy Worters     F. "Sugar Jim"
7. _____ Frank McCool     G. "Shrimp"
8. _____ Ken Dryden     H. "The Cat"

# 6

# WEARING THE COLOURS

On February 4, 1997, Ray Bourque surpassed Johnny Bucyk as the Boston Bruins' all-time points leader. Owning an NHL team's career scoring record is a remarkable distinction for a defenseman. During his long career in Beantown, the modest and hardworking Bourque has been a class act, both on and off the ice. No one has ever worn the Bruins' black, gold and white with more distinction. To honour Bourque, in this chapter we explore some hockey traditions, records and oddities associated with wearing a team's colours.

*(Answers are on page 63)*

6.1 **Why did goalie Ed Belfour choose to wear No. 20 after he was traded to San Jose in 1996-97?**
   A. It was the number he wore in college hockey
   B. It was his age when he joined the NHL
   C. It was the number of shutouts he had in his career
   D. It was a tribute to his former goalie coach

6.2 **Which 1990s expansion team retired the number of a player who never played for them?**
   A. The Ottawa Senators
   B. The Florida Panthers
   C. The San Jose Sharks
   D. The Tampa Bay Lightning

6.3 **Which NHL team introduced a new third jersey in 1996-97, with a woman's image on the crest?**
   A. The St. Louis Blues
   B. The New York Rangers
   C. The Philadelphia Flyers
   D. The Vancouver Canucks

**6.4** Who holds the career mark for most games played in a Toronto Maple Leafs uniform?
A. Dave Keon
B. Tim Horton
C. George Armstrong
D. Borje Salming

**6.5** How many different players wore a St. Louis uniform during Mike Keenan's two-and-a-half-year reign as coach and general manager of the Blues?
A. 52
B. 62
C. 72
D. 82

**6.6** What symbol was on the front of the Montreal Canadiens jersey during the club's founding years, 1910-1914?
A. A "CH," like today
B. A hockey stick
C. A maple leaf
D. A flaming torch

**6.7** Which NHL player bought his own junior hockey team in 1996?
A. Steve Yzerman
B. Patrick Roy
C. Brett Hull
D. Brian Leetch

**6.8** Which of these Hall of Famers was *never* the captain of an NHL team?
A. Bobby Hull
B. Marcel Dionne
C. Doug Harvey
D. Phil Esposito

**6.9** Which of the Original Six teams had to wait the longest before one of its players won a scoring title?
A. The Boston Bruins
B. The Chicago Blackhawks
C. The New York Rangers
D. The Detroit Red Wings

**6.10** Who is the only player to post a 100-point season for an NHL team that recorded less than 20 wins?
A. Quebec's Joe Sakic
B. Hartford's Ron Francis
C. St. Louis' Bernie Federko
D. Pittsburgh's Mike Bullard

**6.11** On December 1, 1996, the Canucks' Trevor Linden sprained a knee, ending his league-leading streak of 482 consecutive games. How many games was Linden short of Doug Jarvis's NHL iron-man record?
A. Exactly one-quarter of Jarvis's total
B. Exactly half of Jarvis's total
C. Exactly three-quarters of Jarvis's total
D. Only one game short of Jarvis's total

**6.12** Who holds the record for playing the most consecutive games for one NHL team?
A. Buffalo's Craig Ramsay
B. Detroit's Alex Delvecchio
C. St. Louis' Gary Unger
D. Chicago's Steve Larmer

**6.13** In 1990, the Buffalo Sabres retired Gilbert Perreault's No. 11. Why did Perreault wear No. 11?
A. It was picked for him by a fortune-teller
B. It was his number in junior hockey
C. It was the same number as his birthdate
D. It was Buffalo's winning lottery number in the 1970 entry draft

6.14  Who was player-agent Brian Cook referring to when he said, in 1996-97, "I always wanted to represent a player whose jersey would someday hang in the rafters. But unfortunately, in the Bruins' case, I think they wanted to hang it with _____ still in it."
A. Rick Tocchet
B. Bill Ranford
C. Adam Oates
D. Kevin Stevens

# WEARING THE COLOURS
## *Answers*

6.1  **D. It was a tribute to his former goalie coach**
It's been a long time since an NHL goaltender last wore No. 20. But when Belfour was traded from the Blackhawks to the Sharks in 1996-97, he abandoned his customary No. 30 and adopted the unconventional No. 20 to honour Tretiak, the legendary Russian puck stopper. Tretiak, who wore No. 20 for the Soviet Red Army Team, made headlines in 1972 with his brilliant play against Canada in the Summit Series. After his retirement, Tretiak became Belfour's goalie coach in Chicago. Belfour clearly benefited from the Russian's instruction. In his first NHL season, 1990-91, he won the Vezina Trophy as top goalie, the Calder Trophy as rookie of the year, the Jennings Trophy for the best goals-against average and was named to the first All-Star team.

6.2  **A. The Ottawa Senators**
The Senators retired No. 8, which was worn by "Fearless" Frank Finnigan, who played with the old Ottawa Senators from 1924 to 1934. Finnigan scored the first goal of the game in which Ottawa won its last Stanley Cup in 1927. As the last surviving member of that championship squad, Finnigan lived long enough to be on hand when Ottawa was granted a new NHL franchise in 1990. He also learned that his old No. 8 would be retired before the team's home opener. Had Finnigan not died

on Christmas day in 1991, at age 91, he would have dropped the first puck to open the second chapter in the history of his beloved Senators.

### 6.3   B. The New York Rangers
The Rangers' new third jersey, which was introduced in 1996-97, received mostly positive reviews. Its crest featured the crowned visage of Lady Liberty emblazoned above the letters NYR. The idea of using the famous landmark originated with Ranger president and general manager Neil Smith. "We wanted a look that was identifiable with New York, and the Statue of Liberty was a better choice than, say, the Empire State Building," said Smith.

### 6.4   C. George Armstrong
Armstrong was dubbed "Chief," partly because of his mother's Iroquois heritage and partly because Alberta's Stoney Indian tribe christened him "Big-Chief-Shoot-the-Puck" when Armstrong's Allan Cup-winning senior club made a western tour. In 1957-58, he became the ninth and last Leaf captain to be personally appointed by Toronto president and general manager Conn Smythe. In 1971, the Chief retired, having proudly worn the blue-and-white for 21 seasons. His 1,187 games is a Leaf record, just two games more than the previous record holder, Tim Horton, who was traded to the Rangers in 1969-70.

### Toronto's Most-Games-Played Roster*

| Player | GP | G | A | PTS | PIM |
|---|---|---|---|---|---|
| George Armstrong | 1,187 | 296 | 417 | 713 | 721 |
| Tim Horton | 1,185 | 109 | 349 | 458 | 1,389 |
| Borje Salming | 1,099 | 148 | 620 | 768 | 1,292 |
| Dave Keon | 1,062 | 365 | 493 | 858 | 75 |
| Ron Ellis | 1,034 | 332 | 308 | 640 | 207 |
| Bob Pulford | 947 | 251 | 312 | 563 | 691 |

*Current to 1997

## 6.5    D. 82

They may as well have installed a revolving door in the Blues'
dressing room during Keenan's two-and-a-half-year St. Louis
tenure. A total of 82 players wore the Bluenote; many didn't
stay long enough to get their uniforms dirty. Keenan's compul-
sive trading habits cost him his job. Dealing draft picks, dis-
carding fan favourites such as Brendan Shanahan and Curtis
Joseph, and unloading skill players for plodding muckers such
as Adam Creighton, Craig McTavish, Greg Gilbert, Mike
Peluso and Stephane Matteau didn't turn the Blues around, but
it did drive fans away. Season ticket renewals dropped to 85 per
cent from 97 per cent and attendance declined by 3,000 per
game. The growing alienation of the Blues' fans and Keenan's
ongoing feud with star Brett Hull finally prompted management to hand Iron Mike his pink slip in December 1996.

## 6.6    C. A maple leaf

Talk about the unthinkable—a maple leaf on a Montreal Canadiens jersey! Say it ain't so. Hockey's most storied franchise, the
Canadiens, not once but twice wore the emblem of their greatest rivals, the Maple Leafs. When George
Kennedy purchased the Club Canadien in
1910, he had the new red uniform emblazoned with a green maple leaf and a
gothic "C." A year later, the Canadiens
got their new "barber pole" model
with blue, white and red stripes.
Again, the sweater had a small
maple leaf crest (in white) with
the letters "CAC," for Club
Athletique Canadien. It was not
until 1916 that the Canadiens'
famous emblem—a large "C"
surrounding a small "H"—was
adopted. Of course, Toronto's
familiar maple leaf crest was not
worn until Conn Smythe bought
the club in 1927.

### 6.7  B.  Patrick Roy

Along with partners Michel Cadrin and Jacques Tanguay, Roy (who played junior hockey with the Granby Bisons) purchased the Beauport Harfangs in December 1996 for $750,000. "Through my career, a lot of good things have happened," said Roy. "I had the chance to play in the American Hockey League and win a Calder Cup. And I've won three Stanley Cups in the NHL. But I've never won the Memorial Cup. This is my objective." Roy's dream could take awhile to become a reality. The Harfangs, whose name means Owls, failed to make the playoffs during 1996-97, Roy's first season as owner.

### 6.8  A.  Bobby Hull

Hull was never appointed captain in the NHL. During his many years with Chicago, the "C" was worn by Ed Litzenberger, Pierre Pilote and Pat Stapleton. Hull split his final NHL season (1979-80) between Winnipeg and Hartford. The Jets' captain was Lars-Erik Sjoeberg and the Whalers' captain was Don Blackburn. As for Phil Esposito: he captained the Rangers for three years in the late 1970s; Marcel Dionne was captain of the Red Wings in 1974-75; Doug Harvey wore the "C" for Montreal in 1960-61.

### 6.9  D.  The Detroit Red Wings

After entering the NHL in 1926-27, Detroit would wait 23 years before one of its players captured a scoring title. Ted Lindsay finally broke the drought in 1949-50, when he scored a league-high 78 points on 23 goals and 55 assists. Placing second and third in the scoring derby were Lindsay's linemates, Sid Abel and Gordie Howe, as the Wings soared to first place and captured the Stanley Cup.

### 6.10  A.  Quebec's Joe Sakic

No one was more deserving of success with Colorado than captain Joe Sakic. During the franchise's lean years in Quebec, Sakic was virtually a one-man band. He is the only player to register a 100-point season for an NHL team with less than 20 wins in a season. Incredibly, Sakic did it twice, scoring 109 points in 1990-91, when the Nordiques had 16 wins, and 102 points in 1989-90, when they won 12 games.

## Most Player Points on 20-Win Teams*

| Player | Year | Team | Wins | G | A | PTS |
|---|---|---|---|---|---|---|
| Joe Sakic | 1990-91 | Que | 16 | 48 | 61 | 109 |
| Joe Sakic | 1989-90 | Que | 12 | 39 | 63 | 102 |
| Bernie Federko | 1978-79 | StL | 18 | 31 | 64 | 95 |
| Mike Bullard | 1983-84 | Pit | 16 | 51 | 41 | 92 |
| Ron Francis | 1982-83 | Hfd | 19 | 31 | 59 | 90 |
| Wilf Paiement | 1977-78 | Col | 19 | 31 | 56 | 87 |

*Current to 1997

### 6.11  B.  Exactly half of Jarvis's total

An innocent-looking collision with Flyer big gun John LeClair on December 1, 1996, damaged the medial collateral ligament in Linden's left knee and ended his NHL-leading iron-man streak. The Canucks captain had played 482 straight games, exactly half of Doug Jarvis's record total of 964. Amazingly, Jarvis didn't miss a game after making his NHL debut on October 8, 1975, until his retirement on October 10, 1987.

### 6.12  D.  Chicago's Steve Larmer

A contract dispute early in the 1993-94 season ended Larmer's record streak. The right-winger had played 884 consecutive games with Chicago from October 6, 1982, to April 16, 1993. Larmer's iron-man streak broke Craig Ramsay's mark of 776 straight games for Buffalo.

### 6.13  D.  It was Buffalo's winning lottery number in the 1970 entry draft

When Buffalo and Vancouver entered the NHL in 1970, league officials decided which expansion team would get the first draft pick by spinning a roulette wheel. The Canucks chose the low numbers (1-8), while the Sabres had the high numbers (9-16). The wheel stopped at 11. Buffalo picked the premier junior player, Gilbert Perreault. Recognizing an auspicious omen when he saw one, Sabres general manager Punch Imlach gave Perreault uniform No. 11. Perreault wore it with great honour for 17 seasons before retiring in 1987 as Buffalo's all-time scoring leader.

## 6.14 C. Adam Oates

On February 18, 1997, Oates publicly vented his frustration with Boston's management, saying, "I"m sick of it. We're not talented enough. We're getting worse every year. I think the problem is upstairs. They're not doing their job." The Bruins' assistant general manager Mike O'Connell responded by accusing Oates of being a selfish player. He insisted Oates' criticism was inspired by frustration over his contract rather than concern over the club's direction, and stripped Oates of his alternate captaincy. A few weeks later, Oates was dealt to Washington.

# GAME 6

# NHL TEAMS

In this puzzle, find the names of all 26 NHL clubs from the 1996-97 season by reading across, down or vertically. Like our example, San Jose S-H-A-R-K-S, connect the names using letters no more than once. Start with the letters printed in heavy type.

*(Solutions are on page 115)*

```
W H A S S K A H K C B S
S E K I L T W R S A L N E D
P A M A N E A V I L I R I W
T N I S L G R E D U S L I N
H L S L R F S S R R E A O G
E A Y E F E G B A R L E N S
S R N R S L M N S A N H P C
S C D F S I S I V G S A H E
N O E A G A B A G U R E S U
E R Y E H N R S I H N K-S L
I S O L T E I C N U T A C B
S D T E S C N A K C N Y D U
M E A L A G I P S A T E K C
A P N S L A T S R O S S
```

69

# 7

# TRUE OR FALSE?

Hockey great Eddie Shore was once asked to describe old-time hockey. "It was pretty much a 50-50 proposition," said Shore, "you socked the other guy and the other guy socked you." This chapter is also a 50-50 proposition. Each statement is either true or false. There are no maybes. Be careful though, as good as these odds are, even the pros sometimes miss a wide-open net with the goalie down and out.

*(Answers are on page 72)*

7.1 Wayne Gretzky and Mario Lemieux have never met in a Stanley Cup playoff game. *True or False?*

7.2 The Hart Trophy, awarded annually to the NHL's MVP, has never been won by a player from a last-place team. *True or False?*

7.3 A goal does not count if the puck enters the net after deflecting off a referee or linesman. *True or False?*

7.4 Bobby Orr's 1966-67 Topps rookie card is the most valuable regular-issue hockey card produced since 1950. *True or False?*

7.5 No player has ever scored 70 goals in a season and not been elected to either the first or second NHL All-Star team. *True or False?*

7.6 A goalie can't be the captain or alternate captain of an NHL team. *True or False?*

7.7 No NHL player has ever been part of *two* club transfers (i.e., Winnipeg to Phoenix). *True or False?*

7.8 Brett Hull was the first St. Louis Blues player to net 50 goals in a season. *True or False?*

70

7.9 Mario Lemieux never scored an overtime playoff goal during his career. *True or False?*

7.10 On average, the NHL has the highest-priced tickets in North American professional team sports. *True or False?*

7.11 The Toronto Maple Leafs have never retired any of their players' numbers. *True or False?*

7.12 No player has ever topped the NHL in points and penalty minutes in the same season. *True or False?*

7.13 Don Cherry, former coach and TV's best-known hockey commentator, never played in the NHL. *True or False?*

7.14 Tampa Bay's Roman Hamrlik was the first European player to be selected first overall in the NHL Entry Draft. *True or False?*

7.15 No team with a losing record in the regular season has ever won the Stanley Cup. *True or False?*

7.16 At one time, the NHL allowed three assists to be awarded on a goal. *True or False?*

7.17 Glenn Hall owns the Chicago Blackhawks club record for most career shutouts. *True or False?*

7.18 No NHL goalie has ever posted more than 20 shutouts in a season. *True or False?*

7.19 There is no goaltender with more than 70 career shutouts who is not in the Hall of Fame. *True or False?*

7.20 The last man to win the Lady Byng Trophy as the NHL's most gentlemanly player with 0 PIM was a defenseman. *True or False?*

7.21 No team has won the Stanley Cup without having home-ice advantage in at least one playoff series. *True or False?*

7.22 Mario Lemieux is the only player to win back-to-back Conn Smythe Trophies as playoff MVP. *True or False?*

7.23 There has never been a penalty shot called in overtime of the Stanley Cup playoffs. *True or False?*

7.24 Wayne Gretzky was *not* the first player selected when he entered the Junior A draft in 1977. *True or False?*

7.25 Guy Lafleur owns the Montreal Canadiens club record for most career goals. *True or False?*

7.26 Prior to winning the Stanley Cup in 1997, the Detroit Red Wings had gone 42 years without a Cup victory, the longest drought of any team in NHL annals. *True or False?*

# TRUE OR FALSE?
## *Answers*

7.1 True
As of 1997, the NHL's two greatest scorers had never opposed one another in a playoff game. Prior to Gretzky's move to the Rangers, the year they had the best chance of meeting was 1993, when Gretzky led the Los Angeles Kings to the finals. But Lemieux's Penguins, the best overall regular-season team, were upset by the Islanders in the Patrick Division finals.

7.2 False
Although it's difficult to imagine it happening today, two players have won the Hart with last-place teams. Tommy "Cowboy" Anderson, a defenseman with the cellar-dwelling Brooklyn Americans, was voted MVP in 1942; goalie Al Rollins won the Hart with the last-place Chicago Blackhawks in 1954. Mario Lemieux captured the award with the Pittsburgh Penguins in 1988—who finished last in the Patrick Division—but Pittsburgh was not the NHL's worst team that year.

**7.3  True**

Although play is not normally halted if a puck deflects off a referee or linesman, Rule 82 of *The Official Rules of the NHL* states: "If a goal is scored as a result of being deflected directly into the net off an official, the goal shall not be allowed."

**7.4  False**

Orr's Topps rookie card from 1966-67 is valued at a startling U.S.$2,500 in mint condition, but it still ranks second in dollar value to Gordie Howe's 1951-52 Parkhurst card, which is listed at U.S.$3,000. Wayne Gretzky's 1979-80 O-Pee-Chee rookie card is listed at U.S.$900.

**7.5  False**

Centre Bernie Nicholls of Los Angeles was not voted to either the first or second NHL All-Star team in 1989, despite racking up 150 points on 70 goals and 80 assists to place fourth in league scoring. Mario Lemieux and Wayne Gretzky, who ranked one-two in the points parade, claimed the two All-Star centre positions.

**7.6  True**

Six NHL goaltenders have served as team captain, but all did so in hockey's early days. The last to wear the "C" was Montreal's Bill Durnan in 1947-48. That year, Durnan's habit of leaving his crease to question calls by the referee drew the ire of opposition teams, who claimed that his actions slowed the pace of the game and gave the Habs unscheduled time-outs at strategic intervals. As a result, the NHL passed a rule in 1948-49 prohibiting goalies from captaining teams.

**7.7  False**

It is rare that a player finds himself in Curtis Leschyshyn's position. In 1995, the veteran Quebec Nordiques defenseman became a member of the Colorado Avalanche after the club's transfer to Denver. Then, in November 1996, Leschyshyn was traded to Washington and a week later to Hartford. The Whalers relocated in 1997, guaranteeing Leschyshyn a place in hockey lore.

**7.8 False**

The first St. Louis player to net 50 goals was right-winger Wayne Babych, who scored 54 times in 1980-81. It was the only time in Babych's nine-year NHL career that he topped the 30-goal mark.

**7.9 True**

At the time of his retirement in 1997, Lemieux had racked up more regular-season overtime goals than any other NHLer, yet oddly enough he had never potted one in the playoffs. Lemieux's not the only superstar in this category. Gordie Howe never scored in a playoff overtime either.

**7.10 True**

The NHL's average ticket price in 1996-97 was $38.34. This made it the costliest in professional team sports: almost $3 higher than the average NFL ticket, $7 more than the average NBA ticket and $27 more than the average Major League Baseball ticket.

**7.11 False**

Toronto has retired only two numbers—Bill Barilko's No. 5 and Ace Bailey's No. 6. The Leafs have also created a special "honoured" number category, which includes No. 1 (Turk Broda and Johnny Bower); No. 7 (Tim Horton and King Clancy); No. 9 (Ted Kennedy); and No. 10 (Syl Apps). The honoured numbers stay in circulation and are commemorated by a special shoulder patch, which current players wear on their jerseys.

**7.12 True**

No scoring champion has ever led the NHL in penalty minutes, but a couple have come close. Nels Stewart paced the league in scoring in 1925-26 and accumulated 119 PIM, just two minutes less than league-leader Bert Corbeau. In 1949-50, Ted Lindsay topped the loop with 78 points while racking up 141 PIM, just three minutes less than the NHL's top bad guy, Bill Ezinicki.

**7.13 False**

Cherry had the briefest of NHL careers. It lasted exactly one game. On March 31, 1955, he played defense for the Boston

Bruins in the fifth game of the Stanley Cup semifinals versus the Canadiens at the Montreal Forum. The Bruins lost 5-1 and were eliminated from the playoffs. Cherry played in the minors until 1971-72, but he never got another taste of the NHL as a player.

## 7.14 False
In 1989, Quebec made history by selecting Swedish star Mats Sundin first overall in the NHL Entry Draft.

## 7.15 False
Two teams have won the Cup after recording losing seasons—the 1938 Chicago Blackhawks and the 1949 Toronto Maple Leafs. The Hawks' triumph in 1938 was a real shocker. Chicago's win-loss-tie record was a pathetic 14-25-9.

## 7.16 True
According to James Duplacey in *The Rules of Hockey*, "From 1930-31 to 1935-36, a maximum of three assists could be awarded for any goal. However, because forward passing from zone to zone was not allowed, the instances of three assists being awarded was rare." The two-assists limit was introduced in 1936-37; forward passing from one zone to another became legal with the introduction of the centre redline in 1943-44.

## 7.17 False
Even though Glenn Hall racked up an impressive total of 51 shutouts for Chicago, he still ranks a distant second to Tony Esposito's franchise mark of 74 goose eggs.

## 7.18 False
In 1928-29, the Canadiens' George Hainsworth posted an amazing 22 shutouts in the 44-game schedule. Hainsworth allowed just 43 goals in 44 games for a 0.98 GAA. No other NHL goalie has registered more than 15 shutouts in a season.

## 7.19 False
Lorne Chabot's exclusion from the Hockey Hall of Fame is mystifying. Chabot's 73 career shutouts ranks eighth on the

all-time list, just behind Tony Esposito. His career 2.04 GAA is the fourth-best ever and his playoff average of 1.50 GAA in 37 games ranks third. In his 11-year NHL career, Chabot won Stanley Cups with New York in 1928 and Toronto in 1932, and copped the Vezina Trophy as top goalie with Chicago in 1935. Regarded as a hothead (he was once suspended for punching a goal judge), Chabot was traded five times, which may have diminished his stature in the voters' eyes. But there is no disputing his superb numbers. His absence from the Hall is a clear injustice.

## 7.20 True

Although Bill Quackenbush never spent more than 17 minutes in the penalty box in any of his 13 NHL seasons, he was no cream puff. The burly rearguard was known for his bruising but clean body checks. In 1949, with Detroit, Quackenbush became the first D-man to win the Lady Byng Trophy as the NHL's most gentlemanly player, and the last player to win the award with 0 PIM.

| The NHL's Penalty-Free Lady Byng Winners* | | | | | | | |
|---|---|---|---|---|---|---|---|
| Player | Year | Team | GP | G | A | P | PIM |
| Syl Apps | 1941–42 | Tor | 38 | 18 | 23 | 41 | 0 |
| Bill Mosienko | 1944–45 | Chi | 50 | 28 | 26 | 54 | 0 |
| **Bill Quackenbush** | **1948–49** | **Det** | **60** | **6** | **17** | **23** | **0** |

*Current to 1997

## 7.21 False

The New Jersey Devils won 1995's Stanley Cup despite not having home-ice advantage in any of the four series in which they played. The Devils posted a record 10 road victories, winning three times at Boston, twice at Pittsburgh, three times at Philadelphia and twice at Detroit.

## 7.22 False

Philadelphia's Bernie Parent was the first NHLer to bag back-to-back Conn Smythe Trophies. Parent captured the coveted hardware in 1974 and 1975 as he backstopped the Flyers to consecutive Stanley Cups.

**7.23 False**

Among the 31 penalty shots awarded in playoff action between 1937 and 1997, only one has come in overtime. It happened in the second overtime period of game four of the 1996 Pittsburgh-Washington quarterfinals. During a goalmouth scramble, Pens defenseman Chris Tamer knocked the net off its moorings, an infraction which calls for an automatic penalty shot. The Caps selected Joe Juneau to take the shot but goalie Ken Wregget stopped him cold. The overtime lasted another 45 minutes before Petr Nedved scored to give Pittsburgh a 3-2 victory.

**7.24 True**

Despite his goal-scoring exploits in minor hockey and the Junior B ranks, Gretzky was actually selected third in the 1977 Ontario Junior A draft. The Oshawa Generals, who picked first, chose Tom McCarthy; the Kitchener Rangers, with the second pick, took Paul Reinhart. The Sault Ste. Marie Greyhounds, who drafted third, chose the 17-year-old Gretzky, who lit up the OHL in his rookie season, scoring 182 points in 64 games.

**7.25 False**

Although Guy Lafleur scored more NHL goals than Maurice Richard, he ranks second to the Rocket in goals scored in a Montreal Canadiens uniform. Richard notched 544 regular-season goals for the Habs, 17 more than Lafleur. When he retired after the 1959-60 season, Richard was also the NHL's all-time goal-scoring leader. That record no longer belongs to him, but the Canadiens' career goal-scoring mark still does.

**7.26 False**

For long-suffering Detroit fans, the Red Wings' 42-year drought between Stanley Cups may have felt like an eternity, but it ranks second on the all-time futility chart. Prior to capturing the Cup in 1994, the New York Rangers had gone an incredible 54 years without sipping champagne from Lord Stanley's silver chalice.

# GAME 7

# PUCK BUCKS

Ballooning salaries have skyrocketed NHL payrolls, pushing NHL team averages in 1996-97 to a staggering $22.9 million. During 1996-97 there were 185 players earning million-dollar paychecks, an average of seven millionaires per squad. Long gone are the days when Gordie Howe, hockey's best all-round player, unintentionally held salary levels down by not demanding more than a token $1,000 annual increase to his meagre $20,000 pay.

Obviously, today's players are better compensated, not only in wages, signing bonuses, deferred income and marketing fees, but also in fringe benefits. As Ranger general manager Neil Smith says, "There was a time when the players went for the money and we (management) listened. Now that everybody pays, they want to be traded to a contender, and we listen. What's next? Do they want to go where they can get a tan?"

In this game, we pull out the balance sheets to report the bottom line on team salaries. Guess which clubs below match the annual payrolls in the right column.

*(Solutions are on page 116)*

| Anaheim | Boston | Buffalo | Chicago |
| Calgary | Colorado | Dallas | Detroit |
| Los Angeles | Montreal | New York | Phoenix |
| Philadelphia | Pittsburgh | Tampa Bay | |

| | NHL Team | Annual Payroll |
|---|---|---|
| 1. | _____ | $14.5 million |
| 2. | New York Islanders | $14.6 million |
| 3. | _____ | $15.4 million |
| 4. | Edmonton Oilers | $15.8 million |

| | NHL Team | Annual Payroll |
|---|---|---|
| 5. | _____ | $16.0 million |
| 6. | Ottawa Senators | $16.9 million |
| 7. | _____ | $18.3 million |
| 8. | Toronto Maple Leafs | $18.4 million |
| 9. | _____ | $19.6 million |
| 10. | Florida Panthers | $20.1 million |
| 11. | _____ | $21.3 million |
| 12. | _____ | $22.0 million |
| 13. | Hartford Whalers | $22.0 million |
| 14. | _____ | $22.8 million |
| 15. | San Jose Sharks | $22.8 million |
| 16. | _____ | $22.8 million |
| 17. | _____ | $24.0 million |
| 18. | New Jersey Devils | $26.1 million |
| 19. | Vancouver Canucks | $26.4 million |
| 20. | _____ | $27.1 million |
| 21. | Washington Capitals | $27.2 million |
| 22. | _____ | $28.1 million |
| 23. | St. Louis Blues | $29.2 million |
| 24. | _____ | $31.1 million |
| 25. | _____ | $34.7 million |
| 26. | _____ | $37.9 million |

# 8

## READER REBOUND

In our last book, we again invited readers to send us their own trivia questions for publication. The response was overwhelming. Unfortunately, we can only publish the top 20. Thanks to everyone for playing. If you want to join next year's Reader Rebound, fill out the form at the back of this book.

*(Answers are on page 82)*

**8.1** Which two teams have met in the Stanley Cup playoffs the most times?

*Ryan Liddell*
*Hamilton, Ontario*

**8.2** Which undrafted player holds the record for scoring the most points by a rookie in one playoff year?

*Janet Fogal*
*Port Huron, Michigan*

**8.3** Who was the first American-born player to post a 50-goal season in the NHL?

*Frank Cardinale*
*West Hempstead, New York*

**8.4** Who was the first NHLer to score 60 goals in a season?

*Josh Getzoff*
*Philadelphia, Pennsylvania*

**8.5** What was Hall of Fame goalie Harry Lumley's nickname?

*Ryan Katchky*
*Thornhill, Ontario*

8.6 Every Soviet player in the 1972 Summit Series wore a helmet, but only one player for Team Canada did. Who was he?

*Steve O'Brien*
*St. John's, Newfoundland*

8.7 Who is the only woman to play for an NHL team?

*Jeni Bohlken*
*Loves Park, Illinois*

8.8 Who was the first Colorado Avalanche player to net a hat trick?

*Kim Nguyen*
*Arvada, Colorado*

8.9 Who holds the record for scoring the most points in one play-off series?

*Dennis Glenn*
*Chipman, New Brunswick*

8.10 The NHL All-Rookie Team has been selected since 1982-83. Who is the only player to be voted NHL rookie of the year and not be elected to the team?

*Ron Aylward*
*Mississauga, Ontario*

8.11 Who scored the first goal in New York Ranger franchise history?

*Brian Schultz*
*Holbrook, New York*

8.12 Besides Wayne Gretzky, which NHLer scored the most points during the 1980s?

*Matt Loch*
*Macomb, Michigan*

8.13 How many names are engraved on the Stanley Cup?

*Anna Hermanson*
*Kingsley, Indiana*

**8.14** Who holds the NHL record for most points in a single game?

*Nathan Inch*
*St. Catharines, Ontario*

**8.15** Which Colorado Rockies player was given a penalty for kissing the puck?

*Danny Watts*
*West Milford, New Jersey*

**8.16** Why was there no winner in the fourth game of the 1988 Stanley Cup finals between Edmonton and Boston?

*Sonia Pannu*
*Victoria, British Columbia*

**8.17** Which 1967 expansion team made the Stanley Cup finals three years in a row?

*Greg Kuperman*
*New City, New York*

**8.18** Which NHL team had the most 20-goal scorers in one year?

*Joe Sgambelluri*
*Weston, Ontario*

**8.19** Who was the NHL's first scoring champion?

*Ryan Johnston*
*Brampton, Ontario*

**8.20** How many holes are there in a hockey net?

*Elizabeth Normand*
*St. Lambert, Quebec*

# Reader Rebound
## *Answers*

**8.1** **The Montreal Canadiens and Boston Bruins** have waged war in the NHL playoffs more than any other pair of teams. As of 1997, these bitter rivals had met 28 times, with Montreal holding a big edge in series play, having defeated Boston 21 times. Second on the list are Detroit and Toronto, with 23 playoff matchups.

**8.2** The Minnesota North Stars staged a major upset by making the Stanley Cup finals in 1981. One of the club's most surprising performers was freshman **Dino Ciccarelli**, who collected 21 points on 14 goals and seven assists to set a new record for points by a rookie in one playoff year. Ciccarelli was not drafted by any NHL team. Minnesota signed him as a free agent on September 28, 1979.

**8.3** **Bobby Carpenter** lit the lamp 53 times for Washington in 1984-85, to become the first American-born player to post a 50-goal season in the NHL. The native of Beverly, Massachusetts, was also the first American-born player to jump directly from high school hockey to the NHL, joining the Capitals in 1981-82, at age 17.

**8.4** Filling the net was **Phil Esposito**'s specialty. In 1970-71, the Bruins sniper became not only the NHL's first 60-goal man, but the league's first 70-goal man as well. Esposito destroyed Bobby Hull's record of 58 goals in a season by scoring 76 times.

**8.5** His rosy-hued complexion earned Harry Lumley the nickname "**Apple Cheeks**." Lumley tended the nets for four different NHL teams from 1943-44 to 1959-60. His best seasons were spent in Toronto, where he won the Vezina Trophy in 1954 with a 1.86 GAA and 13 shutouts, and was named a first-team All-Star in 1954 and 1955. Lumley was elected to the Hall of Fame in 1980.

**8.6** The only Team Canada player to wear a helmet in the 1972 Summit Series was scoring star **Paul Henderson**. Few NHLers wore helmets at the time, but it was fortunate for Canada that Henderson did. During the seventh game of the series, he whacked his head on the boards after taking a nasty spill. Without the helmet he likely would have suffered a concussion and been out of the lineup for game eight. As it was, Henderson played and scored the last-minute game winner, considered by many to be the most famous goal in hockey history.

**8.7** Goalie **Manon Rheaume** became the first woman to play for an NHL team when she appeared between the pipes for the Tampa Bay Lightning in an exhibition game against the St. Louis Blues on September 23, 1992. Rheaume played one period and allowed two goals on nine shots.

**8.8** Initially, some Colorado fans questioned the 1995 trade that brought **Claude Lemieux** to the Avalanche for Wendel Clark. But after being inserted on a line with Peter Forsberg and Valeri Kamensky, Lemieux quickly established himself as one of Colorado's most effective forwards. On November 28, 1996, he netted three goals in a 7-3 win against the Islanders to post the Avalanche's first hat trick.

**8.9** The NHL record for most points in a playoff series was set by Boston's **Rick Middleton** in 1983. The shifty forward sliced and diced the Buffalo Sabres' defense for 19 points on five goals and 14 assists in the seven-game Adams Division finals.

**8.10** This is a weird one. How does a Calder Trophy winner not make the NHL All-Rookie Team? Apparently, only if his name is **Pavel Bure**. Since both the rookie of the year and the members of the All-Rookie team are chosen by members of the Professional Hockey Writers Association, you would expect some consistency in the balloting. Yet in 1992, the media reps voted in schizophrenic fashion, picking Bure as the NHL's top rookie, but selecting Tony Amonte instead of the Russian Rocket as the All-Rookie team's right-winger. The two other forward spots were claimed by rookies Kevin Todd (centre) and Gilbert Dionne (left wing).

**8.11** More than 13,000 fans jammed Madison Square Garden on November 16, 1926, to witness the New York Rangers first game in the NHL. The Rangers' opponents on this historic night were the Montreal Maroons, the defending Stanley Cup champs. The Rangers defeated the Maroons 1-0 on a goal by captain **Bill Cook** at 10:37 of the second period. Cook went on to lead the NHL in scoring in 1926-27 and the Rangers finished atop the NHL's American Division.

**8.12** Wayne Gretzky was easily the dominant scorer of the 1980s, amassing 1,842 points for the decade. However, some may be surprised to learn that the next most prolific scorer of the 1980s was not one of Gretzky's Oiler teammates, but rather Quebec Nordiques sniper Peter Stastny, who compiled 1,059 points on 385 goals and 674 assists.

| The 1980's Top Point Scorers | | | |
|---|---|---|---|
| **Player** | **Goals** | **Assists** | **Points** |
| Wayne Gretzky | 626 | 1,216 | 1,842 |
| Peter Stastny | 385 | 674 | 1,059 |
| Jari Kurri | 474 | 569 | 1,043 |
| Denis Savard | 351 | 662 | 1,013 |
| Paul Coffey | 283 | 669 | 952 |
| Mark Messier | 368 | 569 | 937 |
| Dale Hawerchuk | 379 | 550 | 929 |

**8.13** According to the Hockey Hall of Fame, as of 1997 there are **almost 2,000 names** engraved on the Stanley Cup. The current trophy does not include all the names. Some of the inscribed bands that encircle its barrel have been retired and placed in storage in the Hall.

**8.14** On February 6, 1976, Maple Leaf owner Harold Ballard publicly criticized his team's slumping captain, **Darryl Sittler**. One day later, at Maple Leaf Gardens, Sittler staged an offensive display that has never been equalled. Sittler scored six goals and added four assists for a record 10 points as the Leafs thrashed Boston 11-4. "It was amazing," said the Bruins' Andre Savard after the game. "It was like his shots were directed by radar."

The victim of Sittler's outburst was rookie goalie Dave Reece, who was promptly demoted to the minors; he never played in another NHL game. Ballard, suddenly full of praise for his maligned captain, described Sittler's accomplishment as "a greater feat than Paul Henderson's goal in Russia in 1972," and gave him a valuable silver tea set.

**8.15** The Colorado Rockies had never beaten the New York Islanders until the two teams met on November 28, 1979, so **Randy Pierce** was understandably excited when he scored to give the Rockies a 6-4 lead at 19:27 of the third period. Pierce was so thrilled that he impulsively grabbed the puck, kissed it and tossed it into the crowd. He was promptly penalized for delaying the game. Fortunately for Pierce, teammate Wilf Paiement scored a shorthanded goal into the empty net on the ensuing Islanders power play to clinch the win for Colorado.

**8.16** In 1988, for the first time since 1927, a Stanley Cup finals game failed to determine a winner. During the fourth game of the Oilers-Bruins series, **a power failure** at Boston Garden knocked out the lights in the old building and halted play at 16:37 of the second period with the score tied 3-3. When the lights could not be restored, the game was suspended. Under NHL bylaws, the match would be replayed only if a seventh and deciding game was necessary. The Oilers dispensed with that possibility by defeating Boston 6-3 in Edmonton in the next game to sweep the series and clinch the Cup.

**8.17** When the NHL expanded from six to 12 teams in 1967-68, it split into East and West Divisions, with all six expansion teams in the West. The playoffs were conducted within separate divisions until the finals, when the two division champions met to decide the Cup. This insured an expansion team would play an established team in the final round. **The St. Louis Blues**, stocked with veterans and coached by Scotty Bowman, proved to be the class of the newcomers, qualifying for the finals three years in a row. However, the Blues failed to win a single finals game. They were swept twice by Montreal and once by Boston.

**8.18** Although Peter McNab was the only member of **the 1977-78 Boston Bruins** to top the 30-goal mark, the club boasted a record crew of 20-goal scorers. In all, 11 different Bruins notched 20 goals or more. Joining McNab (41 goals) were Terry O'Reilly (29), Bobby Schmautz (27), Stan Jonathan (27), Jean Ratelle (25), Rick Middleton (25), Wayne Cashman (24), Gregg Sheppard (23), Brad Park (22), Don Marcotte (20) and Bob Miller (20).

**8.19** When the NHL was organized in 1917 it intended to grant franchises to five teams, but 10 days before the league's official formation, the Quebec Bulldogs folded and its players were divided up among the other four clubs. The Montreal Canadiens obtained Quebec's top marksman, **Joe Malone**, who starred for the Habs, scoring an amazing 44 goals in 20 games to win the scoring title. The mark lasted until 1944-45, when Maurice Richard scored 50 goals in 50 games.

**8.20** According to Jean Corriveau, foreman at Montreal's Molson Centre, there are approximately 48 square feet of netting covering the top and back of each regulation-size goal net, depending "on how tight you pull the netting." After making some scientific calculations, (in other words, laboriously counting the number of holes per square foot—about 100—and multiplying by 48 square feet), the answer is 4,800 holes. Add one more, for the great big hole between the pipes where the puck enters, and our final tally is **4,801 holes.**

# GAME 8

# TOUGH GUY ALIASES

Most nicknames are unique, as special as the individuals given them. No one but Wayne Gretzky is "The Great One;" "The Roadrunner" could only be little speedster Yvan Cournoyer; and there is only one "Dominator" between the pipes, Dominik Hasek. Then again, the NHL has known a collection of "Reds," "Babes" and "Mooses." In our nickname research, "Joe," an old common name, came up five times with different aliases. Match them up here.

*(Solutions are on page 117)*

| | | | |
|---|---|---|---|
| 1. _____ | Simpson | A. | "Phantom Joe" |
| 2. _____ | Primeau | B. | "Bullet Joe" |
| 3. _____ | Malone | C. | "Gypsy Joe" |
| 4. _____ | Hall | D. | "Bad Joe" |
| 5. _____ | Hardy | E | "Gentleman Joe" |

The 24 players below also share something in common. Although their monikers are unique, each played the tough guy role during their era, and were christened accordingly.

## Part 1

| | | | |
|---|---|---|---|
| 1. _____ | Chris Nilan | A. | "The Albanian Assassin" |
| 2. _____ | Eddie Shack | B. | "Tough Tony" |
| 3. _____ | Tie Domi | C. | "Tiger" |
| 4. _____ | Bill Ezinicki | D. | "Big Al" |
| 5. _____ | Al Secord | E. | "The Entertainer" |
| 6. _____ | Billy Smith | F. | "Knuckles" |
| 7. _____ | Dave Williams | G. | "Wild Bill" |
| 8. _____ | Tony Leswick | H. | "The Hatchet Man" |

## Part 2

1. _____ Dave Schultz A. "Mad Dog"

2. _____ Lou Fontinato B. "Moose"

3. _____ Ivan Irwin C. "Scarface"

4. _____ Andre Dupont D. "King Kong"

5. _____ Ted Lindsay E. "The Hammer"

6. _____ Todd Ewen F. "Animal"

7. _____ Jerry Korab G. "Ivan the Terrible"

8. _____ Bob Kelly H. "Leapin' Louie"

## Part 3

1. _____ John Ferguson A. "Terrible Teddy"

2. _____ Stu Grimson B. "Mr. Elbows"

3. _____ Ken Baumgartner C. "Black Jack"

4. _____ Bobby Schmautz D. "Dr. Hook"

5 _____ Ted Green E. "Fergie"

6 _____ Gilles Marotte F. "Grim Reaper"

7. _____ Jack Stewart G. "Bomber"

8. _____ Gordie Howe H. "Captain Crunch"

# 9

# THE WORLD STAGE

Although the Olympics have featured international competition in hockey since 1920, the first real challenge to Canada's supremacy at the world level came in 1954, when the Soviets made their debut and won the World Hockey Championships in Sweden. At their first Olympics in 1956, the Russians took the gold again, beating the U.S. (silver) and Canada (bronze). Then, in 1960, the Americans won their first Olympic gold medal.

As a prelude to 1972's Canada-Soviet Summit Series, the big red machine won three more Olympics and seven straight world championships. But because they had never faced Canada's best NHLers, few Canadians gave the Tretiaks, Yakushevs and Kharlamovs much credit.

In this chapter we enter the international arena for a look at some of hockey's best moments.

*(Answers are on page 93)*

9.1 Which NHL team had the most players selected to play in the 1996 World Cup?
A. The New York Rangers
B. The Colorado Avalanche
C. The Edmonton Oilers
D. The Montreal Canadiens

9.2 Who scored the winning goal in the 1996 World Cup?
A. Brett Hull
B. Tony Amonte
C. Derian Hatcher
D. John LeClair

**9.3** The World Cup was formerly known as the Canada Cup. Of the five Canada Cup tournaments staged, how many did Canada win?
A. Two
B. Three
C. Four
D. Five

**9.4** Bobby Orr was voted MVP of the 1976 Canada Cup, but, oddly, he was not voted MVP for Team Canada. Who won that honour?
A. Rogie Vachon
B. Guy Lafleur
C. Darryl Sittler
D. Bobby Clarke

**9.5** Many feel that the 1987 Canada Cup was the most dramatic tournament of all. All three games of the championship final between Canada and the Soviet Union finished with an identical score. What was the score?
A. 4-3
B. 5-4
C. 6-5
D. 7-6

**9.6** Whose cross-check on Wayne Gretzky during the 1991 Canada Cup caused the NHL to change its rules and assess an automatic game misconduct penalty to anyone who hits another player from behind?
A. The Soviet Union's Vyacheslav Fetisov
B. The U.S.'s Chris Chelios
C. Sweden's Ulf Samuelsson
D. The U.S.'s Gary Suter

**9.7** Which was the first nation, other than Canada, to win an Olympic Gold medal in hockey?
A. The U.S.
B. The Soviet Union
C. Czechoslovakia
D. Great Britain

**9.8** Who did the U.S. defeat in the final game of the 1980 Olympics at Lake Placid to win the gold medal and complete the "Miracle on Ice"?

A. Sweden
B. Finland
C. The Soviet Union
D. Czechoslovakia

**9.9** Which member of the 1980 U.S. Olympic team had a father who played on the U.S. hockey team that won the Olympic gold medal in 1960?

A. Dave Christian
B. Mike Ramsey
C. Mark Johnson
D. Jim Morrow

**9.10** In 1972, a team of NHL All-Stars met the Soviet Union's National Team for the first time in the famous Summit Series. Who was the top point-getter in the series?

A. Paul Henderson
B. Phil Esposito
C. Valery Kharmalov
D. Alexander Yakushev

**9.11** Why did Bobby Hull not play for Canada in the Summit Series?

A. He was not picked for the team
B. He was injured
C. He had to work on his farm
D. He was not a member of the NHL

**9.12** Who was the surprise visitor who showed up in the Soviet team's dressing room prior to the first game of the Summit Series in Montreal?

A. Canadian prime minister Pierre Trudeau
B. NHL goalie great Jacques Plante
C. Soviet premier Leonid Brezhnev
D. NHL president Clarence Campbell

9.13 The Soviets scored nine power-play goals in the eight games of the Summit Series. How many power-play goals did the Canadian team score?
A. Two
B. Five
C. Eight
D. 11

9.14 Who holds the record for most career points in World Junior Championship competition?
A. Russia's Pavel Bure
B. Finland's Saku Koivu
C. Sweden's Peter Forsberg
D. The Czech Republic's Robert Reichel

9.15 Who scored the overtime winner for Canada at the Woman's World Championships in 1997?
A. Angela James
B. Cassie Campbell
C. Nancy Drolet
D. Hayley Wickenheiser

# THE WORLD STAGE
## Answers

9.1 **A. The New York Rangers**
In all, nine Rangers made the 1996 World Cup roster. The players were Wayne Gretzky, Mark Messier and Adam Graves of Canada; Mike Richter and Brian Leetch of the U.S.; Alexei Kovalev, Sergei Nemchinov and Alexander Karpovtsev of Russia; and Niklas Sundstrom of Sweden.

9.2 **B. Tony Amonte**
A native of Hingham, Massachusetts, Amonte put home a rebound off a point shot from Derian Hatcher to give the U.S. a 3-2 lead against Canada in the third period of the 1996 World Cup. It stood up as the winning marker in Team USA's 5-2 win.

Surprisingly, the goal generated little fanfare in Amonte's homeland: not a single word about his exploits appeared in the Hingham newspaper, evidence of how little impact the World Cup had on the U.S. consciousness. If he had scored the goal during the Olympics, it's likely Amonte would have become a household name.

**9.3    C. Four**
Canada's lone defeat in the Canada Cup occurred in 1981, when the Soviet Union trounced the host country 8-1 in the sudden-death final. Controversy ensued after the game when tournament director Alan Eagleson prevented the Soviets from taking the Canada Cup Trophy home with them. Eagleson claimed that the original trophy had to stay in Canada. The Soviets were given a replica instead.

**9.4    A. Rogie Vachon**
Orr and Vachon were both outstanding in the 1976 Canada Cup. Orr counted nine points on two goals and seven assists tying teammate Denis Potvin and Viktor Zhluktov of the Soviet Union for most points in the tournament. Vachon's stellar goaltending was a key to Canada's victory; he allowed only 10 goals in seven games for a 1.39 GAA.

**9.5    C. 6-5**
The Soviets won game one on a goal by Alexander Semak after five minutes of overtime. In game two, the clubs played 30 minutes of extra time before Mario Lemieux redirected a Wayne Gretzky shot past Soviet goalie Evgeny Belosheikin for the winning goal. In game three, Team Canada fell behind 3-0 and 4-2, rallied to take a 5-4 lead and then lost it. But with less than two minutes left in the game, Gretkzy broke down the left wing, faked out a Soviet defender and slid the puck over to Lemieux, who buried it in the top corner to win the game and the tournament for Canada.

**9.6    D. The U.S.'s Gary Suter**
During game one of the 1991 Canada Cup championship series, Team USA defenseman Gary Suter cross-checked Wayne

Gretzky into the corner boards behind the U.S. net. Gretzky slumped to the ice in pain. Incredibly, no penalty was called on the play. Although he was able to leave the ice under his own power, Gretzky was sidelined for the rest of the series with back spasms. After the incident, Gretzky was dogged by chronic back pain and the condition eventually forced him to miss half of 1992-93. Even though the check was legal, the NHL realized how close the hit had come to ending the career of hockey's premier player. As a result, in 1992, the league began assessing automatic game-misconducts to any player who hits or pushes another player from behind.

**9.7 D. Great Britain**

At the 1936 Winter Olympics, Great Britain's hockey team pulled off a huge upset by defeating Canada to take the gold medal. In the previous four Olympics, Canadian teams had decimated the competition, outscoring their opponents in 17 games by a cumulative tally of 209 to eight. Ironically, the 1936 British team was stocked with Canadian servicemen and renegades, players who were born in Great Britain but raised in Canada. The team's coach, Percy Nicklin, was also a Canadian. Thanks to some spectacular goaltending by Winnipegger Jimmy Foster, Great Britain defeated Canada 2-1 in the medal round. The Canadians expected to get another crack at the British team in the final, but Olympic officials ruled that because Britain had beaten Canada once, a return match wasn't necessary. Even though Canada finished the tournament with a 7-1-0 win-loss record, while Great Britain was 5-0-2, the gold medal went to the British.

**9.8 B. Finland**

The underdog Americans stunned the hockey world in 1980 by defeating the powerhouse Soviet team 4-3, on Mike Eruzione's third-period goal. But that upset occurred in Team USA's second-last game. The Americans had to defeat Finland in the final game to capture the Olympic gold medal, which they did by a score of 4-2.

**9.9 A. Dave Christian**

There were actually two Christians on the U.S. team that won Olympic gold at Squaw Valley in 1960—Dave's father, Bill, and his uncle, Roger. The two brothers were the club's top scorers and counted the key goals in the U.S.'s victories against the defending champion Soviet Union and then versus Czechoslovakia in the final game. Hockey is clearly an all-consuming affair for this Warroad, Minnesota, clan, who are well-known hockey-stick manufacturers.

**9.10 B. Phil Esposito**

Although Paul Henderson scored three game-winning goals for Team Canada, Esposito was the club's best player and inspirational leader. Espo had a hand in all three of the Canada's third-period goals in the dramatic come-from-behind victory in game eight, scoring one and setting up the other two, and he led all series scorers with 13 points.

**9.11 D. He was not a member of the NHL**

Hull had just signed with the Winnipeg Jets of the newly-formed WHA. The NHL viewed the WHA as a threat and was loathe to do anything that would suggest it was accepting the upstart league as its equal. Accordingly, NHL president Clarence Campbell declared that if a single WHA player joined Team Canada, the NHL would bar all of its players from competing in the series. Campbell's announcement outraged Canadians, who demanded that Hull be allowed to play for his country. But in the end the NHL won the showdown and Hull was scratched from the team.

**9.12 B. NHL goalie great Jacques Plante**

An hour before the first game of the series, Vladislav Tretiak looked up from lacing his skates and was shocked to see Jacques Plante, one of his goaltending idols, standing in front of him. The two had met three years earlier. When Tretiak was 17 and visiting Canada with his national junior team, Plante had worked with him on his technique. Plante, who at 43 was still playing in the NHL, was worried how Tretiak would manage.

Tretiak said about the encounter: "He showed me how the Canadians shot the puck. He talked about Cournoyer, Mahovlich, Esposito. I think he felt a little sorry for me. He didn't think I'd do well." That might be a slight understatement considering Plante predicted that Canada would win the series 8-0.

## 9.13   A.  Two
Considering the ineptitude of Canada's power play and the large edge the Soviets enjoyed in power-play chances, the Canadian victory in 1972 is even more miraculous. The Soviets had 38 manpower advantages and scored nine power-play goals. Canada had 23 power-play opportunities and scored just twice.

## 9.14   C.  Sweden's Peter Forsberg
Although Forsberg didn't truly establish himself as an NHL superstar until 1995-96, Colorado's centre had earlier demonstrated his tremendous potential with Sweden's national junior team. At the 1993 World Junior Championship, Forsberg set an all-time tournament record with 31 points in seven games. He ranks first in career points among tournament scorers with 42 points on 10 goals and 32 assists.

## 9.15   C.  Nancy Drolet
Gritty centre Nancy Drolet was Canada's heroine at the 1997 Women's World Championships, scoring a hat trick, including the overtime winner in the dramatic 4-3 win over the U.S. in the final. It was the Canadians' fourth consecutive gold medal at the tournament, but their world supremacy is tenuous. While the Canadians played dump-and-defend hockey all night, the Americans showed speed and finesse. Both teams hit hard, yet Canada was badly outskated. The final game, played April 6, 1997, at Kitchener Memorial Auditorium in Ontario, drew 6,247 fans, the largest attendance ever at a women's game.

# GAME 9

# THE EUROPEAN INVASION

The vast majority of non-North Americans playing in the NHL come from such European countries as Finland, Sweden, the Czech Republic and Russia. The 58 non-North American players listed below appear in the puzzle horizontally, vertically, diagonally or backwards. After you've circled all 58 names (like I-R-B-E), read the remaining letters in descending order to spell the name and the nickname of one of hockey's greatest non-North American scorers from the 1960s.

*(Solutions are on page 118)*

| | | | |
|---|---|---|---|
| ANDERSSON | AUGUSTA | BERG | BICANEK |
| BURE | BYAKIN | CALOUN | CARNBACK |
| CIGER | CZERKAWSKI | DAFOE | DEMITRA |
| DROPPA | DVORAK | ELIAS | GUSAROV |
| HAMRLIK | HASEK | IRBE | JAGR |
| KAPANEN | KARABIN | KARAMNOV | KARPOVTSEV |
| KLIMA | KOHN | KOIVU | KOROLEV |
| KOVALENKO | KOVALEV | KUDASHOV | KURRI |
| LARIONOV | LIDSTROM | LUMME | MALIK |
| MARHA | NAZAROV | NEDVED | PAEK |
| PELTONEN | ROHLIN | SALO | SATAN |
| SELANNE | SEMENOV | SLEGR | STUMPEL |
| SUNDIN | SVOBODA | SYKORA | TITOV |
| ULANOV | VARADA | VOPAT | ZEDNIK |
| ZHITNIK | ZUBOV | | |

```
K I L R M A H R A M A L I K O I V U
A K U I K O V A L E N K O U L B S N
R S M L D E M I T R A R T R E I A A
P W M B A S N M I V O K I R T N M T
O A E K I N T S A L O A G I I N L A
U K V I D C O R E L I A S B E E U S
T R O N T V A V O P A T A N P G E U
S E T T H D O N E M U R A M U L O N
E Z I I A R R R E N A P U S A A F D
V C T H A G C O A K A T T N D R A I
E K A Z E H K H P K S A N E E I D N
L I A L H V C L V P A E K C V O A E
A N S A O B A I O K A A M B D N D N
V D S B L U B N R E C Z R E E O O O
O E U E C R N H A (E B R I) G N V B T
K Z A N D E R S S O N H O K A O O L
V O N M A R A K U D A S H O V J V E
N I K A Y B C I G E R A R O K Y S P
```

# 10

# COUNTDOWN TO THE CUP

Are players superstitious? Ask Ottawa's Ron Tugnutt. He wore the same clothes (and underwear) on game day for a full month leading up to the 1997 Stanley Cup playoffs. "This isn't one of those disgusting stories. My clothes are cleaned every day," said Tugnutt. And it worked. The Senators' netminder won five of seven games to finish the regular season, with three shutouts and a stellar 1.86 goals-against average. Tugnutt's performance fired his teammates to Ottawa's first postseason in modern history. "It's just one of those things that builds as it goes on. You find a comfort zone and it turns into a routine." Oddly, Tugnutt has no special system for his hockey gear. "I couldn't tell you how I put on my equipment. I just do it."

In this chapter, we take a cue from Tugnutt and the Senators, a goalie and a team that emerged from obscurity after four consecutive last-place overall finishes.

*(Answers are on page 104)*

10.1 The Detroit Red Wings' Russian unit played a key role in the team's march to the Stanley Cup in 1997. In how many of Detroit's 16 playoff wins did one of its five Russian players score a point?
   A. In 13 wins
   B. In 14 wins
   C. In 15 wins
   D. In all 16 wins

10.2 Who accused the Philadelphia Flyers of "choking" in the 1997 Cup finals versus Detroit?
   A. Detroit captain Steve Yzerman
   B. Detroit coach Scotty Bowman
   C. Philadelphia coach Terry Murray
   D. Philadelphia general manager Bobby Clarke

10.3 Which of the following playoff goaltending records did Patrick Roy *not* own by the end of the 1997 Stanley Cup playoffs?
A. Most career shutouts
B. Most career playoff wins
C. Most career playoff games
D. The longest shutout sequence in overtime

10.4 What item did the Ottawa Senators use as a rallying symbol during the 1997 playoffs?
A. A letter from a fan
B. An editorial cartoon
C. A smiling Buddha
D. A silver hockey stick

10.5 Which NHL owner accused his club's doctor of mistreating one of the team's star players, and of conspiring to aid the team's opponents during the 1997 playoffs?
A. Philadelphia's Ed Snider
B. Chicago's Bill Wirtz
C. Detroit's Mike Ilitch
D. New Jersey's John McMullen

10.6 League champions don't always prevail in the playoffs. Of all the first-place finishers that failed to win the Cup, which team had the best regular-season winning percentage?
A. The 1929-30 Boston Bruins
B. The 1944-45 Montreal Canadiens
C. The 1970-71 Boston Bruins
D. The 1995-96 Detroit Red Wings

10.7 When the Boston Bruins failed to qualify for the playoffs in 1996-97, it ended a record streak of how many consecutive playoff appearances?
A. 20
B. 23
C. 26
D. 29

10.8 Why was Sergei Fedorov's overtime goal in game six of the 1992 Norris Division semifinals an historic NHL event?
A. It was the fastest overtime goal ever scored
B. It was the first shorthanded goal in overtime
C. It was the first time a video replay was used to decide a playoff game
D. It was the first overtime playoff goal scored on a penalty shot

10.9 Since 1927, how many NHLers have scored a Stanley Cup-winning goal and also coached a Stanley Cup-winning team?
A. No one has ever accomplished both feats
B. One player
C. Two players
D. Four players

10.10 Why was Buffalo Sabres netminder Dominik Hasek suspended and fined during the 1997 playoffs?
A. He refused to attend practice
B. He broke curfew
C. He assaulted his coach
D. He assaulted a sportswriter

10.11 Which NHL owner was taken hostage during the 1982 playoffs by an armed man who demanded $1 million in ransom money?
A. Bill Wirtz of the Chicago Blackhawks
B. Harold Ballard of the Toronto Maple Leafs
C. Jerry Buss of the Los Angeles Kings
D. Peter Pocklington of the Edmonton Oilers

10.12 Beginning in 1951, the Montreal Canadiens embarked on a record-setting streak of consecutive appearances in the Cup finals. How many years in a row did the Habs reach the showdown series?
A. Six
B. Eight
C. 10
D. 12

**10.13** Which was the first city west of Winnipeg to host a Stanley Cup finals?

A. Calgary
B. Edmonton
C. Vancouver
D. Seattle

**10.14** Who holds the record for most career points in the Cup finals?

A. Jean Béliveau
B. Gordie Howe
C. Henri Richard
D. Wayne Gretzky

**10.15** Which is the only NHL team to finish first in the regular season and yet fail to appear in the Stanley Cup playoffs?

A. The 1920-21 Ottawa Senators
B. The 1924-25 Hamilton Tigers
C. The 1929-30 Montreal Maroons
D. The 1941-42 New York Rangers

**10.16** Who owns the NHL record for scoring points in the most consecutive playoff games?

A. Guy Lafleur
B. Bryan Trottier
C. Stan Mikita
D. Wayne Gretzky

**10.17** As of 1997, who is the only player selected first overall in the NHL Entry Draft to win the Stanley Cup during his rookie season?

A. Montreal's Rejean Houle
B. Philadelphia's Mel Bridgman
C. The New York Islanders' Denis Potvin
D. Pittsburgh's Mario Lemieux

# COUNTDOWN TO THE CUP
## *Answers*

**10.1  C.  In 15 wins**

Detroit's talented Russian five—Sergei Fedorov, Slava Kozlov, Igor Larionov, Vladimir Konstantinov and Slava Fetisov—were criticized for not performing up to expectations in the club's disappointing playoff showing in 1996. But no one complained about the quintet's play in the 1997 playoffs. In Detroit's upset of the defending-champion Colorado Avalanche in the Western Conference finals, the Russians scored nine of the Wings' 16 goals. All told, Detroit's playoff record was a dazzling 15-0 when one of its Russian players registered a point. The only Detroit win they did not score in was the 2-1 Cup-clinching victory versus the Flyers. After the game, Larionov said, "I've been playing professional hockey for 20 years and this is the happiest moment in my life. We've got five Russians and I've heard every player gets the Cup for two days. Five times two: 10 days. So we can take it to Russia for the Russian people to enjoy it, to touch it."

**10.2  C.  Philadelphia coach Terry Murray**

With the Flyers trailing the Red Wings three games to none in the 1997 Cup finals, Murray resorted to a risky and unusual psychological ploy, suggesting his team was in the process of choking. While discussing the Flyers' waning confidence level with reporters, Murray said, "I don't know where it has gone. Many teams have been through this problem before and it is basically a choking situation." Philadelphia played better in game four, but still lost, going down in four straight. It was the first time the Flyers had lost four games in a row since March 1993.

**10.3  A.  Most career shutouts**

Roy ended the 1997 postseason with 11 career playoff shutouts, four shy of Clint Benedict's career record of 15. Yet the Colorado netminder, who already owned the mark for most playoff games by a goalie, did add two more records to his résumé during the 1997 playoffs. Roy surpassed Billy Smith's mark of 88 career playoff wins and also set a record for the longest overtime shutout sequence in NHL annals. Roy had blanked opposition shooters for a span of 162 minutes and 56 seconds in sudden death before Chicago's Sergei Krivokrasov finally scored on him, at 11:03 in overtime of game three of Colorado's first-round playoff series. Roy's shutout string eclipsed the standard of 160 minutes and 15 seconds set by Chicago's Charlie Gardiner between 1930 and 1934.

## 10.4   C.  A smiling Buddha

During the 1997 playoffs, fans at Ottawa's Corel Centre were seen brandishing "cheer cards" featuring a smiling Buddha holding the Stanley Cup aloft and the words "Buddha Power." Why Buddha? It all started in January when Senators forward Tom Chorske bought a smiling Budda figurine, with a big round belly and arms stretched high over its head, in a shop in San Jose, Califonia. It was one of four so-called Chinese Buddhas on sale. One represented wealth, one health, one wisdom and one good luck. Chorske picked the one promising good fortune. The keepsake was placed in the Senators' dressing room and soon after Ottawa embarked on a winning surge, which propelled the club to its first-ever playoff berth. But even Buddha power has its limits. The Senators were skewered by the Buffalo Sabres in seven games in their inaugural playoff tilt.

## 10.5   B.  Chicago's Bill Wirtz

As the Colorado Avalanche and Chicago Blackhawks duelled on the ice during the 1997 playoffs, a bizarre medical controversy erupted behind the scenes. Hawks team physician Dr. Louis Kolb resigned during game three after he was berated by Wirtz, who was furious that Kolb had allowed Avalanche team physician Dr. Andrew Parker to perform surgery on the ankle of Hawks centre Alexel Zhamonov—without consulting management. Kolb said he asked Parker to perform the operation in Denver because he did not have the proper licence to do surgery in Colorado, but Wirtz accused Kolb of conspiring with the enemy. The Chicago owner also accused Kolb of mis-diagnosing a Brent Sutter knee injury as a sprain, clearing the veteran centre to play with what was actually a torn ligament.

## 10.6 A. The 1929-30 Boston Bruins

Based on regular-season performance, the 1929-30 Bruins rank as the biggest postseason flop in NHL history. Boston compiled a 38-5-1 win-loss-tie record, collecting 77 of a possible 88 points for a winning percentage of .875. Not even the 1995-96 Detroit Red Wings, who set a record for most regular-season wins, topped that. The Bruins' offense was led by the Dynamite Line of Cooney Weiland, Dit Clapper and Dutch Gainor; their defense was anchored by Hall of Famer Eddie Shore and Vezina Trophy-winning goalie Tiny Thompson. Few believed the Boston juggernaut could be stopped, but the Bruins proved unable to cope with the blinding speed of the Canadiens' Flying Frenchmen. They lost the best-of-three final in two straight games. It was the first time that the Bruins lost back-to-back games all season.

### Best Winning Percentages by Non-Cup Winners*

| Teams | GP | W | L | T | PCT |
|---|---|---|---|---|---|
| 1929-30 Boston Bruins | 44 | 38 | 5 | 1 | .875 |
| 1944-45 Montreal Canadiens | 50 | 38 | 8 | 4 | .800 |
| 1995-96 Detroit Red Wings | 82 | 62 | 13 | 7 | .799 |
| 1970-71 Boston Bruins | 78 | 57 | 14 | 7 | .776 |
| 1985-86 Edmonton Oilers | 80 | 56 | 17 | 7 | .744 |
| 1975-76 Philadelphia Flyers | 80 | 51 | 13 | 16 | .738 |

*Current to 1997*

## 10.7 D. 29

The Bruins' streak of 29 straight playoff appearances is an NHL record, as is their string of 29 consecutive winning seasons. The only team in North American pro sports to have a longer streak is baseball's New York Yankees, who had 39 winning seasons from 1926 to 1964. The last time the Bruins missed the play-offs was in 1966-67, the last year of the six-team era. Boston finished in the NHL cellar that season but their future held great promise, thanks to rookie-of-the-year Bobby Orr. The outlook for the Bruins in 1997 was not nearly so promising.

**10.8  C. It was the first time a video replay was used to decide a playoff game**

In overtime of game six of the Detroit-Minnesota divisional semifinal, the Wings' Sergei Fedorov wired a shot past Stars net-minder Jon Casey that appeared to ricochet off the crossbar. After a stoppage in play, referee Rob Shick consulted with video replay supervisor Wally Harris, who determined that the puck had actually entered the net, giving the Wings a 1-0 victory. It was also an historic goal for another reason—it was the first time a Russian-trained player had scored an overtime goal in the playoffs.

**10.9  D. Four players**

When Jacques Lemaire coached New Jersey to the 1995 Stanley Cup, he became only the fourth player in NHL history to score a Cup winner and coach a Cup champion. Lemaire scored Cup-winning goals for Montreal in 1977 and 1979.

| Player/Coach | Cup Goal Year | Scorer Team | Cup-Winning Year | Coach Team |
|---|---|---|---|---|
| Jacques Lemaire | 1977 | Montreal | 1995 | New Jersey |
| | 1979 | Montreal | | |
| Toe Blake | 1944 | Montreal | | |
| | 1946 | Montreal | 1956-60 | Montreal |
| | | | 1965 | Montreal |
| | | | 1966 | Montreal |
| | | | 1968 | Montreal |
| Frank Boucher | 1928 | New York | 1940 | New York |
| Cy Denneny | 1927 | Ottawa | 1929 | Boston |

**Stanley Cup-Winning Goal-Scoring Coaches***

*Current to 1997*

## 10.10  D.  He assaulted a sportswriter

The NHL slapped Hasek with a three-game suspension and a $10,000 fine for grabbing *Buffalo News* sportwriter Jim Kelley and ripping his shirt after game five of the Sabres-Senators playoff series. Hasek was upset by a column that Kelley had written, in which he questioned the severity of the Buffalo goalie's knee injury. Kelley suggested Hasek's absence from the Sabres' lineup might have more to do with an inability to cope with the pressure of carrying the club's playoff hopes on his shoulders.

## 10.11  D.  Peter Pocklington of the Edmonton Oilers

The Oilers' owner emerged from a bizarre and harrowing hostage-taking drama with a bullet in his arm, but his life intact. The incident began on April 20, 1982, when a masked gunman burst into Pocklington's Edmonton mansion. Pocklington was bound and gagged by the intruder, but his wife, Eva, escaped and alerted police. After a 12-hour stand-off, in which the man demanded $1 million in ransom money and an airplane to take him to an undisclosed location, police stormed the house and fired a shot that passed through the gunman's chest, winging Pocklington in the shoulder. The kidnapper had a pistol pointed at Pocklington's head when he was shot. The wounded man was then taken into custody.

## 10.12  C.  10

The Canadiens went to the big dance 10 straight years, from 1951 to 1960, and won the Cup six times, including an unprecedented five in a row from 1956 to 1960. Chicago ended Montreal's glorious run in six games during the 1961 semifinals, as Glenn Hall blanked the Habs' scoring machine for six straight periods, posting back-to-back shutouts in games five and six.

## 10.13  C.  Vancouver

In 1915, Vancouver became the first city west of Winnipeg to host the Stanley Cup finals, when the National Hockey Association champion Ottawa Senators journeyed west to meet the

Pacific Coast Hockey Association champion Vancouver Millionaires. The best-of-five series was played at Vancouver's Denman Street Arena. The cavernous 10,500-seat arena was the next-largest indoor sports stadium in the world, second only to New York's Madison Square Garden. Built in 1912, at a cost of $300,000, it was a wildly ambitious structure for a city with a population of only 150,000. Spurred on by the sellout hometown crowd, the Millionaires trounced the eastern invaders, 6-2, 8-3 and 12-3. The Denman Street Arena played host to one more Stanley Cup final in 1921. It was destroyed by a fire in 1936.

## 10.14  A.  Jean Béliveau

The great Canadiens centre retired after the 1970-71 season, at age 41. He went out on top, captaining the Habs to the Stanley Cup, the 10th of his illustrious career. Béliveau finished the playoffs with six goals and a then-record 16 assists, leaving the sport as the all-time leader in playoff points. He still holds the mark for most points in the finals.

### Most Career Points in the Finals*

| Player | Games | Goals | Assists | Points |
|---|---|---|---|---|
| Jean Béliveau | 64 | 30 | 32 | 62 |
| Wayne Gretzky | 31 | 18 | 35 | 53 |
| Gordie Howe | 55 | 18 | 32 | 50 |
| Henri Richard | 65 | 21 | 26 | 47 |
| Maurice Richard | 59 | 34 | 12 | 46 |
| Bernie Geoffrion | 53 | 24 | 22 | 46 |
| Frank Mahovlich | 45 | 16 | 25 | 41 |

*Current to 1997*

## 10.15  B.  The 1924-25 Hamilton Tigers

To accommodate two expansion teams in 1924-25, the NHL expanded its schedule from 24 to 30 games. The move sparked the league's first labour dispute. The first-place Hamilton

Tigers refused to compete in the playoffs unless the team received a $200 raise per man as compensation for the six extra games it had played during the season. NHL president Frank Calder rejected the demand and the Hamilton players went on strike. Calder responded by suspending the striking players and fining them each $200. He also decreed that the second- and third-place teams, Montreal and Toronto, would meet to decide the NHL title. The next season, Hamilton's troublesome team was moved to New York, where it was renamed the Americans. Despite several bids, Hamilton has never made it back into the NHL.

### 10.16  B. Bryan Trottier
The New York Islanders' championship squads of the early 1980s boasted a host of talented performers, but none contributed more to the club's success than Bryan Trottier. The hard-driving centre counted a point in 27 consecutive playoff games between 1980 and 1982, setting a record that no other player has approached. Even Wayne Gretzky's point-scoring streak of 19 straight games in 1988 and 1989 is a distant second. Trottier logged 42 points (16 G, 26 A) in those 27 games, but he was especially impressive during the 1981 playoffs, when he scored a point in all 18 games the Islanders played to set a record for the longest consecutive point-scoring streak in one playoff year.

### 10.17  A. Montreal's Rejean Houle
Although number one draft picks Mel Bridgman of Philadelphia (1975) and Florida's Ed Jovanovski (1994) both reached the Stanley Cup finals in their rookie seasons, Houle (1969) is the only top draft pick to win the Cup in his first year. Houle scored three points in 1970's dramatic seven-game Montreal-Chicago championship round.

# SOLUTIONS TO GAMES

## Game 1: JUSTICE FOR ALL

| If ... | got ... | then ... | got ... |
|---|---|---|---|
| Gordie Howe | $205,005; | Gump Worsley | $184,901 |
| Tony Esposito | $ 94,494; | Phil Esposito | $128,002 |
| Larry Robinson | $ 26,841; | Ray Bourque | $ 7,083 |
| Eddie Shack | $125,955; | John Ferguson | $ 59,043 |
| Joel Quenneville | $ 9,961; | Jacques Lemaire | $ 77,465 |
| Serge Savard | $ 90,485; | Denis Potvin | $ 36,376 |
| Gerry Cheevers | $ 86,814; | Eddie Johnston | $148,756 |
| Bryan Trottier | $ 23,544; | Mike Bossy | $ 14,835 |
| Ken Dryden | $ 43,432; | Bobby Orr | $ 69,311 |
| Brian Propp | $ 7,701; | Charlie Simmer | $ 21,612 |
| Jean Béliveau | $132,161; | Bobby Hull | $106,411 |
| Alex Delvecchio | $154,760; | Ron Ellis | $ 91,072 |
| Frank Mahovlich | $121,316; | Stan Mikita | $164,837 |
| Wayne Gretzky | $ 6,917; | Mark Messier | $ 6,917 |

## Game 2: THE ORIGINS OF STARS

### Part 1
1. Joe Sakic     E. Swift Current Broncos (WHL)
2. Keith Tkachuk     F Boston University (HE)
3. Peter Bondra     H. VSZ Kosice (Czech.)
4. Ray Bourque     B. Sorel Eperviers (QMJHL)
5. Eric Lindros     A. Oshawa Generals (OHL)
6. Mike Modano     G. Prince Albert Raiders (WHL)
7. Paul Kariya     C. University of Maine (HE)
8. Pavel Bure     D. CSKA (USSR)

### Part 2
1. Brett Hull     H. University of Minnesota-Duluth (WCHA)
2. Mats Sundin     E. Djurgarden (Sweden)
3. Trevor Linden     G. Medicine Hat Tigers (WHL)
4. Pierre Turgeon     C. Granby Bisons (QMJHL)
5. Keith Primeau     B. Niagara Falls Thunder (OHL)
6. Teemu Selanne     A. Jokerit (Finland)
7. John LeClair     D. University of Vermont (ECAC)
8. Brendan Shanahan     F. London Knights (OHL)

## Game 3: CROSSWORD

```
C   G                             C
R   R                             A
A A N                             N
I   T                             A
G   F                             D
B U P   P L A N T E   P L A S S E I
I H E     A   E     B   I     E   N
L O R N E R O U S S E A U   L     S
I   A     I   F     L   T R A P
N E A L B R O T E N   I       N
G   T     N   L E   V     S N O W
T O N Y   B O R D E L E A U   E   R
O   K     V       L   A           E
N   B I L L   C   Y O U N G   B I G
  R   L   U   O           E     G
G O A L   O G R O D N I C K   R   E
A   E   N   B   A   C   H U R T
C   R   G   E   S   E       B
H E S H O O T S H E S C O R E S
```

112

## Game 4: PENALTY LEADERS

Toronto's R-E-D H-O-R-N-E-R was tough, mean and fearless. Although his career penalty record of 1,254 minutes doesn't approach today's standard, during his era (1929 to 1940) that total went unchallenged. Horner led the NHL in penalty minutes for a record eight straight seasons, beginning in 1932-33.

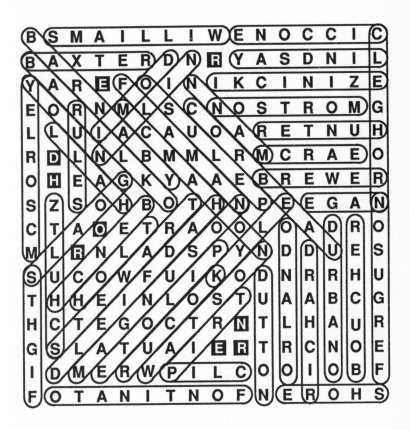

# Game 5: CHICO, GUMP AND JAKE THE SNAKE

## Part 1
1. Dominik Hasek
2. Glenn Hall
3. Chuck Rayner
4. Andre Racicot
5. Terry Sawchuk
6. Georges Vezina
7. Felix Potvin
8. Glenn Resch

C. "The Dominator"
G. "Mr. Goalie"
E. "Bonnie Prince Charlie"
F. "Red Light"
H. "The Shutout King"
D. "The Chicoutimi Cucumber"
A. "The Cat"
B. "Chico"

## Part 2
1. Patrick Roy
2. Billy Smith
3. Cecil Thompson
4. Tony Esposito
5. Michel Larocque
6. Walter Broda
7. Grant Fuhr
8. Gary Smith

B. "St. Patrick"
F. "The Hatchet Man"
E. "Tiny"
G. "Tony O"
D. "Bunny"
C. "Turk"
H. "Cocoa"
A. "Suitcase"

## Part 3
1. John Vanbiesbrouck
2. Gerry Cheevers
3. Jacques Plante
4. Frank Brimsek
5. Steve Buzinski
6. Lorne Worsley
7. Richard Brodeur
8. Johnny Bower

D. "Beezer"
C. "Cheesey"
H. "Jake the Snake"
B. "Mr. Zero"
G. "Puckgoesinski"
A. "Gump"
F. "King Richard"
E. "China Wall"

## Part 4
1. Ed Giacomin
2. Emile Francis
3. Jim Henry
4. Rogatien Vachon
5. Harry Lumley
6. Roy Worters
7. Frank McCool
8. Ken Dryden

E. "Fast Eddie"
H. "The Cat"
F. "Sugar Jim"
C. "Rogie"
D. "Apple Cheeks"
G. "Shrimp"
A. "Ulcers"
B. "The Thinker"

```
W—H—A  S  S—K  A—H—K—C  B  S
S—E  K—I  L  T  W—R—S  A—L  N—E—D
P—A  M—A  N  E  A  V—I—L  I  R  I—W
T—N  I  S  L  G  R  E—D  U  S  L—I  N
H  L—S  L  R  F  S  S  R  R  E  A  O  G
E  A  Y—E  F  E—G  B  A  R  L  E  N  S
S—R  N  R—S  L  M  N  S  A  N  H  P  C
S  C  D  F—S  I  S  I  V  G  S  A  H  E
N  O  E  A  G  A—B  A  G  U  R  E  S  U
E  R  Y  E  H  N  R  S  I  H  N  K—S  L
I  S  O  L  T  E  I  C  N  U  T  A—C  B
S  D  T  E  S  C  N  A  K—C  N  Y—D  U
M  E  A  L  A  G  I—P  S  A  T—E  K—C
A—P  N  S—L—A—T  S—R—O  S  S
```

## Game 7: PUCK BUCKS

| NHL Team | Annual Payroll* |
|---|---|
| 1. Boston Bruins | $14.5 million |
| 2. New York Islanders | $14.6 million |
| 3. Calgary Flames | $15.4 million |
| 4. Edmonton Oilers | $15.8 Million |
| 5. Anaheim Mighty Ducks | $16.0 million |
| 6. Ottawa Senators | $16.9 million |
| 7. Los Angeles Kings | $18.3 million |
| 8. Toronto Maple Leafs | $18.4 million |
| 9. Tampa Bay Lightning | $19.6 million |
| 10. Florida Panthers | $20.1 million |
| 11. Montreal Canadiens | $21.3 million |
| 12. Buffalo Sabres | $22.0 million |
| 13. Hartford Whalers | $22.0 million |
| 14. Chicago Blackhawks | $22.8 million |
| 15. San Jose Sharks | $22.8 million |
| 16. Phoenix Coyotes | $22.8 million |
| 17. Dallas Stars | $24.0 million |
| 18. New Jersey Devils | $26.1 million |
| 19. Vancouver Canucks | $26.4 million |
| 20. Colorado Avalanche | $27.1 million |
| 21. Washington Capitals | $27.2 million |
| 22. Philadelphia Flyers | $28.1 million |
| 23. St. Louis Blues | $29.2 million |
| 24. Detroit Red Wings | $31.1 million |
| 25. Pittsburgh Penguins | $34.7 million |
| 26. New York Rangers | $37.9 million |

*Source: *The Hockey News*

## Game 8: TOUGH GUY ALIASES

### Introduction
1. B.    "Bullet Joe" Simpson
2. E.    "Gentleman Joe" Primeau
3. A.    "Phantom Joe" Malone
4. D.    "Bad Joe" Hall
5. C.    "Gypsy Joe" Hardy

### Part 1
1. Chris Nilan       F.  "Knuckles"
2. Eddie Shack       E.  "The Entertainer"
3. Tie Domi          A.  "The Albanian Assassin"
4. Bill Ezinicki     G.  "Wild Bill"
5. Al Secord         D.  "Big Al"
6. Billy Smith       H.  "The Hatchet Man"
7. Dave Williams     C.  "Tiger"
8. Tony Leswick      B.  "Tough Tony"

### Part 2
1. Dave Schultz      E.  "The Hammer"
2. Lou Fontinato     H.  "Leapin' Louie"
3. Ivan Irwin        G.  "Ivan the Terrible"
4. Andre Dupont      B.  "Moose"
5. Ted Lindsay       C.  "Scarface"
6. Todd Ewen         F.  "Animal"
7. Jerry Korab       D.  "King Kong"
8. Bob Kelly         A.  "Mad Dog"

### Part 3
1. John Ferguson     E.  "Fergie"
2. Stu Grimson       F.  "Grim Reaper"
3. Ken Baumgartner   G.  "Bomber"
4. Bobby Schmautz    D.  "Dr. Hook"
5. Ted Green         A.  "Terrible Ted"
6. Gilles Marotte    H.  "Captain Crunch"
7. Jack Stewart      C.  "Black Jack"
8. Gordie Howe       B.  "Mr. Elbows"

## Game 9: THE EUROPEAN INVASION

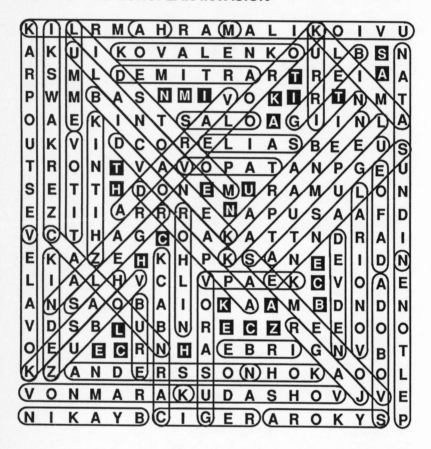

S-T-A-N M-I-K-I-T-A, "T-H-E U-N-C-H-E-C-K-A-B-L-E C-Z-E-C-H" as he was sometimes called, was the first Czechoslovakian-born player in the NHL.

# ACKNOWLEDGEMENTS

Thanks to the following publishers and organizations for use of quoted material:

From *The Hockey News*, various excerpts. Reprinted by permission of *The Hockey News*, a division of GTC Transcontinental Publishing, Inc.

From *The Gazette*. Copyright © Printed and published in Montreal by Southam, Inc.

From *The Rules of Hockey* by James Duplacy. Copyright © 1996 by NHL Enterprises, Inc. and Dan Diamond and Associates, Inc.

Care has been taken to trace ownership of copyright material contained in this book. The publishers will take any information that will enable them to rectify any reference or credit in subsequent editions.

The authors gratefully acknowledge the help of Phil Prichard and Craig Campbell at the Hockey Hall of Fame; Steve Dryden at *The Hockey News*; Jean Corriveau at Molson Centre; Ron Reusch and Peter Schaivi at CFCF 12 in Montreal; the staff at the McLennan-Redpath Library of McGill University; Robert Clements at Greystone Books; the many hockey writers and broadcasters who have made the game better through their own work; as well as editor Anne Rose, fact checker Allen Bishop, graphic artist Ivor Tiltin, puzzle designer Adrian van Vlaardingen and inputter Candice Lee.

# HOCKEY TRIVIA'S READER REBOUND

Do you have a favourite hockey trivia question that stumps everyone, or one that needs an answer? Write us, and if we haven't used it before, we may include your question in next year's trivia book. We can only pick about 20 questions and answers, so give us your best shot.

We'll make sure every question selected is credited with the sender's name and city. Just two points: 1) Duplications will be decided by the earliest postmark; and 2) Sorry, we can't answer letters individually.

**Write us at:** *Hockey Trivia*
*c/o Don Weekes*
*P.O. Box 221*
*Montreal, Quebec*
*Canada*
*H4A 3P5*

**PLEASE PRINT**

NAME: _____ AGE: _____

ADDRESS: _____

FAVOURITE TEAM: _____

FAVOURITE PLAYER(S): _____

YOUR QUESTION: _____

_____

_____

_____

_____

ANSWER: _____

_____

_____

_____

_____

*(continued on next page)*

**Even if you don't have a trivia question,
we'd like to hear from you.**

## READER SURVEY

In future books on hockey trivia, would you like questions that are:

❐ Easier     ❐ About the same     ❐ Harder?

Would you like:     ❐ more games; or     ❐ fewer games?

What kinds of questions or games do you like the most, or would you like more of? (i.e., multiple choice, true or false, fill-in-the-blanks, crosswords, etc.)?

_____

_____

_____

_____

_____

_____

### OTHER COMMENTS:

_____

_____

_____

_____

_____

_____

_____

# THE OPINION CORNER

What do you like most about hockey? _____

_____

_____


How would you like the game to change (i.e., shootouts, two refer-

ees, etc.)? _____

_____

_____


When and how did you first get interested in hockey? _____

_____

_____